Cowboys & Bleeding Hearts

Essays on Violence, Health and Identity

For Joanne
generosity through alms.
Best regards
Ron.

Books by Ron Charach

The Big Life Painting

Someone Else's Memoirs

The Naked Physician

Past Wildflowers

Petrushkin!

Dungenessque

Elephant Street

Selected Portraits

Cowboys & Bleeding Hearts:

Essays on Violence, Health and Identity

by Ron Charach

Wolsak and Wynn

Cover image: John Brown/Olga Korper Gallery
Cover design: Ken Priestley
Author's photograph: Dan Roitner
Typeset in Utopia, printed by Ball Media, Brantford, Canada
Book design: Julie McNeill, McNeill Design Arts

The publishers gratefully acknowledge the support of the Canada Council for the Arts, the Ontario Arts Council and the Book Publishing Industry Development Program (BPIDP) for their financial assistance.

The Canada Council for the Arts | Le Conseil des Arts du Canada

ONTARIO ARTS COUNCIL
CONSEIL DES ARTS DE L'ONTARIO

Canadian Heritage | Patrimoine canadien

The author gratefully acknowledges the support of the Canada Council.

Wolsak and Wynn Publishers Ltd.
#102 69 Hughson Street North
Hamilton, ON
Canada L8R 1G5

Library and Archives Canada Cataloguing in Publication

Charach, Ron
Cowboys & bleeding hearts : essays on violence, health and identity / Ron Charach.

Includes bibliographical references and index.
ISBN 978-1-894987-35-6

1. Social problems. 2. Violence–Social aspects. 3. Jews–Identity. I. Title.

HN18.3.C55 2009 361.1 C2009-900059-8

Printed in Canada

To my mother, Doris Slotnikov Charach,
alevah hashalom (may she rest in peace),
and to the mothers of all victims of
gun violence and addiction.

I write to keep from going mad from the contradictions
I find among mankind – and to work some of those
contradictions out for myself.

MICHEL DE MONTAIGNE

What do I think of Western Civilization?
I think it would be a very good idea.

MOHANDAS GANDHI

The well-adjusted make poor prophets.

ERIC HOFFER

You need imagination in order to imagine
a future that doesn't exist.

AZAR NAFISI

Table of Contents

Introduction: Life & Its Daily Exits 11

Section One: Gun Violence

"When a Good Man Turns Gunman" / Letter to the Editor 19
"American Gun Laws Partly to Blame for this Tragedy" 21
Arms and the Man
Part One: Guns and the Value of North American Lives 22
Part Two: Guns and Maleness 27
Pop, Pop, Pop: The Sound of Violence 36
The Trouble with Tasers 39
Guns, Lethality and the Big Lie 45
Love, Death and Old Men 50

Section Two: Health

"The Art of Psychiatry" 57
Can Lassie Afford to Get Medical Help? 58
A Post-Mortem on Body Worlds 2 60
Death at Arm's Length 65
Mythic Marijuana 68
Masters of Their Universe 80
How Pernicious is Pornography? 89
Adventures in Alternative Medicine 96
"So, Why Do You Write?" 106
Down in the Dark: Poetry in Psychiatry 112
Poets on Prozac: Mental Illness, Treatment and the Creative Process 118

Section Three: Religion & Identity

Rise of Fundamentalism is Scary 123
Fresh Thinking Needed on Mideast 125
Cowboy Nation 126
Don't Call Me White 131
Canaries in the Mind-shaft 138
Shame, Rage and Mideast Violence 144
Reflections on Jewish Identity 152
Borat's Inner Jew 164
The Chutzpah of Atheists 167

Acknowledgements 172
Notes 174
Bibliography 179
Index 183

Introduction: Life & its daily exits

Concerned that my poetry books were reaching no more than a few thousand readers and making no money for me or anyone else, my older brother Arthur would push, "Ronnie, you're a psychiatrist, too. Why not write a self-help book?"

He had a point. Psychiatrists have indeed written inspirational books. One thinks of Karl Menninger, Rollo May, Erich Fromm and the occasional anti-psychiatrist like R. D. Laing, whom a colleague of mine once tried to comfort when the great Scottish psychiatrist broke out in bitter tears at a seminar he gave on birth trauma. I was in the room, and memorialized the incident in a poem, called "R. D. Laing."

The more nitty-gritty business of daily self-help, however, has been largely left to psychologists, to the occasional inspirational figure like Tony Robbins and to physician writers like Deepak Chopra who try to blend Western wisdom with more Eastern approaches. There has also been a flurry of prosy but practical books stemming from Aaron Beck's relatively new discipline of cognitive therapy.

A book of essays and letters hardly passes as self-help, except that in writing them, I am trying to help myself make sense of what has gone awry in North American society and abroad. Almost titled Cowboys & Liberals, this book is the culmination of some twenty years of writing letters to Canadian and American newspapers, urging that society do a better, saner job at controlling lethal agents like firearms, while also taking a closer look at how highly addictive activities might be affecting the readiness of our youth to emerge as the leaders of tomorrow. I also examine the common motivations that affect both psychological healers and writers, and the interface between these two remarkable callings.

There is nothing clinically insane about stocking one's home with semi-automatic weapons in full working order, or even about advocating that young children, their teachers and their grandparents are schooled in the use of and have ready access to such deadly weapons. There is nothing clinically insane about children and teenagers spending five or six hours at a stretch at first-person shooter (FPS) or role-playing video game, or devoting each weekend to bouts of smoking marijuana. Nor are 'physical culturalists' insane when they devote several hours each day to pursue optimal physical health. There is nothing robustly sane about such behaviour, either.

I am indebted to a recent book by British psychoanalyst Adam Phillips, called *Going Sane,* in helping me better understand what I'm really trying to do with a book like this. Psychiatrists and poets are often stereotyped in movies as being a bit wingy and knee-jerk liberal in their politics. Alternatively, they may be portrayed as uptight normality salesmen, eager to step in and take away people's freedoms. They are often vilified for controversial treatments like shock therapy, but receive begrudging respect for their socially necessary role of having to testify on issues of insanity.

Dr. Phillips would urge us to develop a concept of what it might mean to be more deeply, effectively sane. This is not the same as being 'normal' and the greatest task with which a human being can be charged is to remain sane in an insane place or at an insane point in our history. Many of the Bush administration's delayed responses to the truly perverse attacks that occurred on 9/11 seemed to share the confusion that accompanied those attacks.

An old joke, quoted by Freud, describes a Liberal as "a man with his feet firmly planted in mid-air." I am not that kind of liberal. I hope, in this book, to temper my subjectivity with compelling facts drawn from more scholarly and evidence-based sources, while being open about my inner moral compass.

I am intrigued by the emerging view in neuropsychology advanced by Yale psychology professor Paul Bloom, that "each of us contains multiple selves – all with different desires, and all fighting for control." Some of these selves are longer-term and have long-term goals, while others, which arise in the context of, say, pleasure-seeking behaviour and addictions, are shorter-term and have more short-term, sometimes self-destructive goals. Those who set social policy have to consider whether and how to help steer their citizens towards longer-term behaviours that are in the best interests of society, while maintaining adequate respect for the rights of individuals to make choices. Nowhere do such issues loom larger than in areas in which governments feel moved to act to limit lethal agents, from speeding and street racing to cigarettes and alcohol to possession of unequivocally deadly agents like toxins, exotic pets and firearms designed to wound or kill multiple human beings.

While I set to work writing this introduction, world events began to unfold at a feverish pace, from the Wall Street meltdown to the Mumbai terrorist attacks to the Israeli incursion into Gaza, each of which had very personal resonance for me, not only as a psychiatrist preoccupied with the need to make the world a safer, saner place, but as a father, a Canadian and a liberal-minded Jew. I cannot read any newspaper article without these perspectives coming into play, though I try, as an occasional author of non-fiction, to remain aware of these biases as I do my best to evaluate new developments.

Given that this book was compiled immediately post-Bush, but is still, in a sense, pre-Obama, let me start with a letter to *The Toronto Star*, published about the time I completed the final draft of the essays in this book. I should mention that, after writing this, I regretted any aspersion I may have cast on the singularly successful and self-effacing star, Perry Como.

Re: Regrets, he's had a few
Letter to the Editor
(*The Toronto Star*, January 2008)

Thank you for the six full-colour mug shots of President George W. Bush. Your headline, from the song "My Way," written by Canadian Paul Anka, recalls Frank Sinatra, another man thought to have had flexible principles, as in his rumoured links with the Mob.

However, I think the singer that ought to come to mind as a comparison to Bush is Perry Como, whose hits include "Hot Diggity," "Catch a Falling Star" and "Dream on Little Dreamer." Like the soporifically smooth Mr. Como, Bush lulled us into accepting the material he let others write for him.

I like best the quote wherein Bush "readily concedes that (he) chucked aside some of (his) free-market principles," because it seems to me that chucking aside principles, especially on hard-core matters like the permissibility of torture, is very much what Mr. Bush is about. He has certain doctrinaire preferences, it's true, but he is, fundamentally, not all that serious a person; a fatal flaw in the man chosen to lead the free world.

Mr. Bush may be allowed to simply exit, stage right, pardoning his accomplices as he goes. Or there could yet be some sort of truth and reconciliation commission to hold him, Dick Cheney and Donald Rumsfeld to account, and make a really big deal about all those unnecessary casualties and exiles from the pointless, illegal war in Iraq.

In the area of domestic gun control alone, enough has been

> dismantled under Bush's watch as to result in many more American fatalities at home, likely for decades to come. Mr. Bush's genius is his inveterate charm, and I don't know if the attention span of the American public is quite up to freezing the action and fully reviewing the sequence of just how so much was allowed to go so wrong.

Cowboys & Bleeding Hearts was completed in first draft on the eve of the 2008 American presidential election, whose result was pending. I gathered together these essays and letters during the last gasps of Bush's "category five" presidency, while much of the world prayed that the American people might make Barack Obama the country's first biracial president and give him a chance to chart a new course for the free world.

As the ballots were being counted, I wondered if I might have to rewrite some of the essays, depending on whether Barack Obama or John McCain became the forty-fourth president of the United States. Then I remembered that the laws of human nature do not change very quickly. You do not have to be a conservative to acknowledge that.

Consider *Cowboys & Bleeding Hearts* as a call for action to reduce lethal elements in our society, particularly the rapid-fire guns that add a multiplier effect to human misery. It was inspired locally by the shooting of a Toronto mother, Louise Russo, in a Toronto sandwich shop, and by the slaying of eleven-year-old Ephraim Brown in his own neighbourhood, fifteen-year-old Jordan Manners in his own school and fifteen-year-old Jane Creba out shopping with her friends on Boxing Day. More broadly, there were the mass killings that took place at Columbine High School, L'École Polytechnique, Virginia Tech and Dawson College, to name but a few. My determination to speak out multiplied when I learned that a young Brazilian man shot fleeing London police, who had mistaken him for a terrorist, had taken six bullets to the head. I began to suspect that the lively new weapons churned out by the gun companies might be as much to blame as overly zealous police officers, and that the same issues might apply to tasers, which, as I had suspected, are overpowered, unreliable and overused.

The book also issues a call for people, especially young people, to consider where they are headed, and to reconsider the seductive, petty addictions that pull them away from engagement with the wider community. Many of these addictions are propagated through electronic media. There is now a lively debate about how the exposure of infants and young children to hours of television affects their developing brains. There are investigations into whether hours of television exposure might be correlated with the tenfold increase in diagnosed attention-deficit syndromes. The question, then, as to what hours spent in closed-loop addictive diversions might do to a young person's core sense of reality is as much worth asking as how it might impact on his or her values.

Some of these essays highlight identity and race, traits of people which should enrich our social fabric but can also be seized on by some to divide us. I am enamoured of ethnicity and race, and would not want us all to magically blend into the same kind of person, in a world where we all spoke English or Esperanto to each other. I also believe, along with Freud, that human beings have a built-in need to aggress against each other and a moral duty to keep those aggressions minor. Growing up Jewish in the North End of Winnipeg, I learned to do cut-ups of many different accents, including a rich array of Jewish accents. Like Canadian comedian Russell Peters, I celebrate the diversity of our backgrounds, but also find the ethnic mosaic a rich source of humour. While I am not averse to seeing a movie like *Borat* or *Religulous,* I am also aware that, at any moment, presumed differences between groups can become no laughing matter. These differences can be exaggerated to the point of inspiring hate speech and even physical attack.

When I wrote the essays on the need for better gun control, I did not yet know that terrorist attacks on Mumbai would usher in American Thanksgiving. Their savagery was a terrible tragedy for the embattled peoples of India and Pakistan, and marked a turning point in world terrorism, since the attackers, in lieu of bombs, used the very kind of automatic weapons that now saturate the world. The young men involved in the Mumbai attacks functioned as a determined death cult, willing to die and willing to kill at point-blank range, in the most up-close and personal way. They killed Indians who were Hindu as well as their fellow Muslims. They killed foreigners for being foreign and, I feel compelled to add, Jews for being Jews.

As I contemplate their blind belief in the decadence and depravity of Western ways, I think about today's youth, and the mounting challenges they face to reverse a level of savagery in the world that has changed little over the centuries. Beheadings and throat-slitting still occur in Iraq and even Mexico, where gangs cut out each others' tongues. Rape is still the handmaiden of war, especially in Africa, which is already struggling with HIV/AIDS.

Many of our youth do seem up to the task of facing an unsettled future. Many I chat with are concerned about the environment. They understand the need for the wealthier nations to readjust to more "sustainable" ways of living in a world of rapidly depleting natural resources. Yet how ready are they to accept the torch we pass them, given how hard it is to pry themselves from a mind-numbing array of addictive drugs and entertainments? Are the addicted the same people prone to other psychological disorders? Or can anyone get sucked into addictive spirals if the stimuli are sufficiently powerful or incessant? Early on, author Neil Postman wondered if we might be "amusing ourselves to death."

My focusing on marijuana, video games and pornography is rather arbitrary. I could have instead written on binge drinking, thought to affect nearly half of all young drinkers, or about addiction to heroin and the controversies around social policies geared to treating heroin or cocaine addicts. My criticism of the lapse in entertainment standards in the admittedly educational exhibition Body Worlds 2 would apply even more so to the gladiatorial excesses of Ultimate Fighting Championships.

Alas, I chose these specific vices to write about based partly on my own experience. As a psychiatrist, I am an outsider with privileged insights into the drug or computer-driven preoccupations that I hear about from my patients. Nor am I entirely a stranger to periods of excess, but rather, can also sing these words from Paul Simon's song "The Boxer," "I do declare there were times when I was so lonesome, I took some comfort there."

My intention is not to hurl the cynic's ban, but rather to help increase mindfulness about how we spend our time and with what we fill our beleaguered minds. I want to address these questions without becoming too much of a scold. I do not relish becoming what Freud described as "an injustice collector," yet every time I learn of a new shooting, I cannot help but pay close attention to *just how many bullets* were fired; when I hear of an addictive habit, I ask *just how many hours* of a person's day it consumes, and to what extent it waylays their plans or their ambitions.

In the perilous wake of the Bush presidency, after The Bonfire of Junk-Bond Inanities, and in the face of zealous enemies who denounce our relatively easy, free-wheeling way of living, we would do well to focus on these issues.

Section One

Gun Violence

"When a Good Man Turns Gunman"

Letter of the Day
(*The Toronto Star*, September 1994)

"Ban crime, not guns!" cry the gun lobbyists (*The Toronto Star*, September 23, 1994).

But, like their counterparts in America, they underestimate the plasticity of human personality.

Things aren't so cut and dried; it isn't just bred-in-the-bone immoral men who misuse guns. Good men can (and do) become bad men, especially when drunk, too paranoid, too depressed, too jealous or, dare we say it, too desperately poor. And when they have access to guns, their human frailties can rapidly become human tragedies.

Frequently in the US news we hear of some "good enough" man – perhaps a disgruntled postal worker, a depressed student or a laid-off fast food cook – walking into his former workplace or school and shooting up a bunch of people. Dazed witnesses always say, "How could anyone who was so (agreeable, likeable, quiet, nondescript) *possibly* do this? What could have 'gotten into him?'" – the viral theory of human psychopathology.

It is time for gun lobbyists to stop the simple talk about Good Guys versus Bad Guys and stop pressing their governments to allow so many people to keep guns at home.

Letter to the Editor
(*The Toronto Star*, July 2008)

Let's hope your article on knife violence in the UK doesn't lead some handgun fancier to protest that if people can't kill each other one way, they'll just pick another. While, for example, Glasgow's murder rate of 4.3 per one hundred thousand does not compare favourably with Toronto's murder rate of 1.9 per one hundred thousand, even Scotland looks like a peaceable kingdom when contrasted with the murder rate in American cities, where guns instead of knives mean multiple bullets, drive-by shootings and crossfire deaths. Compare, for example, Detroit at 47.3 per one hundred thousand; Baltimore at 43.3 and New Orleans, Newark, St. Louis and Oakland, all with a murder rate of 37 per one hundred thousand, according to 2006 statistics. It is fascinating that the same risk factor of father absence that afflicts Toronto housing projects seems equally true of housing projects in the UK.

"American Gun Laws Partly to Blame for this Tragedy"

Letter to the Editor
(*The Seattle Times,* September 2008)

Whatever the mental illness Isaac Zamora had, it certainly didn't interfere with his marksmanship: The laxity of American gun laws gave this highly dysfunctional man's anger the power to extinguish the lives of several of his betters ("6 dead in Skagit County shooting rampage," *The Seattle Times,* September 3).

Shame on the Republican Party for eight years of dismantling or challenging nearly every gun-control provision possible.

Shame on them for exempting the large gun manufacturers from lawsuits surrounding the criminal negligence with which they market their products.

Zamora's violence never needed to become so all-powerful.

It's time Americans stopped asking themselves "Why?" and started asking the question, "How?"

I have many relatives and close friends who live in the US, and completed my psychiatric training there, but I would never want to be a practicing psychiatrist in a country where so many people are encouraged to store guns in their homes.

Arms and the Man

Part One: Guns and the Value of North American Lives

American epidemiologists are mad as hell and they're not going to take it any more. Who ever thought this presumably docile group would wade into the Great Gun Debate – and in the premiere medical journal of the United States? Perhaps trauma surgeons were fed up of fishing for bullets in the bodies of children and teens. Physicians would no longer sit back while the Bush administration and its ideologically stacked court encouraged law after law harming the best interests of the American public.

The July 31, 2008, issue of *The New England Journal of Medicine* featured the essay "Guns and Health." In it, authors Drazen, Morissey and Curfman called the *District of Columbia v. Heller* Supreme Court decision "a risky epidemiological experiment" about which they could predict no favourable result. They pointed out that in 2005, the last year for which there is data, thirty thousand deaths and seventy thousand non-fatal injuries were caused by firearms in the United States, and that a quarter of the non-fatal injuries and a tenth of the deaths were of children and adolescents. They noted that during the restrictive handgun ban in DC, there was a 25% decline in homicides and suicides by firearms, while no such decline existed in adjacent areas that lacked restrictive laws.

In "Guns and Suicide in the United States," a September 4, 2008 Perspective piece in *The New England Journal of Medicine,* authors Miller and Hemenway made an equally powerful plea: "The Supreme Court's finding of a Second Amendment right to have a handgun in the home does not mean that it is a wise decision to own a gun or to keep it easily accessible. Deciding whether to own a gun entails balancing potential benefits and risks. One of the risks for which the empirical evidence is strongest, and the risk whose death toll is greatest, is that of completed suicide."

The authors' powerful table of "Data on Suicides in States with the Highest and Lowest Rates of Gun Ownership, 2001–2005" ought to freeze gun proliferation advocates in their tracks. These researchers examined the relationship between rates of household gun ownership and suicide in each of the fifty states during a two-year period, using a large telephone survey of more than two hundred thousand respondents. Results were controlled for rates of poverty, urbanization, unemployment and mental illness, as well as drug and alcohol dependence and abuse. They found that "Among men, among women, and in every age group (including children), states with higher rates of household gun ownership had higher rates of firearm suicides and overall suicide."

Don't blame such modern public health findings on the Constitution's Founding Fathers. How could they have foreseen the current era of semi-automatic handguns, in which a distraught student at Virginia Tech, armed with two handguns and ammunition clips, functioned as a one-man militia, killing thirty-one others as well as himself in the worst civilian massacre ever on American soil? Their emphasis on the right of a citizen to bear arms in his own defence came long before what epidemiologic data showed about a loaded gun. In the home, its use is 22% more likely in the suicide of its owner or his teenage son, in a family homicide or an accidental wounding of a child than in self-defence. Nor did they foresee the era of "home-use tasers" and pit bull breeding. Although these last measures are also risky and likely ill-advised, they ought to make even the most anxious homeowner feel protected.

The assumption that all self-defence is completely rational contradicts what we know about the prevalence of mental illness in the general population. While home-handgun owners claim to be law-abiding, they hardly constitute a "well-regulated militia." Too often, they are isolated individuals sceptical about their tax dollars being spent on social programs to help the poor. They may be xenophobic and harbour racist beliefs. As their actions show, many do not trust the government any more than the local police to protect their families. They are as prone as anyone else to jealousy, bitter divorce, job loss and uncontrolled rage. Among their ranks are some of the tens of thousands of American troops returned from rotations in Iraq showing signs of post-traumatic stress disorder (PTSD), for which most receive inadequate treatment. Such experts with firearms are at heightened risk for both suicide and violent acts. Surely, the *District of Columbia v. Heller* decision was not written with these soldiers and their vulnerable families in mind.

As a Canadian psychiatrist who trained for just two years in the United States, in child and adolescent psychiatry, why react so personally to the American Supreme Court ruling on *District of Columbia v. Heller?* I have many relatives and friends in the United States whose lives are precious to me. The landmark narrow ruling that enshrines the right of most American civilians to store loaded guns in their homes values abstract rights over actual human lives. It also synchronizes with the Bush administration's message to the American public over the past eight years: that the government in Washington is elitist and untrustworthy. Therefore, they ought to take the defence of their lives and property into their own hands. This same world view led to decisions as diverse as Florida's "Stand Your Ground" legislation, Oklahoma's consent for students with permits to bring their guns to campus and Harrold, Texas' encouragement for teachers to carry loaded sidearms. More than eighty thousand residents of Galveston, Texas, decided to stand their ground in the face of Hurricane Ike, which they were warned could spell "certain death." In my view, they shared deep cynicism about the government's willingness and ability to be responsible for their safety and overall well-being.

The metaphor of group amnesia may be more to the point. Did a returning Vietnam veteran and his sidekick actually hold the entire capital area hostage for weeks, shooting some eighteen people at random? Did a deranged man really pepper the White House with bullets, and yet another open fire with an automatic rifle inside the Capitol building? The American judiciary clearly lacks a long collective memory.

According to a recent documentary on the Canadian Broadcasting Corporation's *The Fifth Estate,* of more than eighty thousand gun dealerships in the United States, a mere 1% sold more than half of all the guns used in crimes. These gun shops are located in places with the laxest gun laws, such as Georgia, Baltimore, Indianapolis and Tacomah, Washington. Typically, they sell multiple guns to single individuals, who then run the guns north along Interstate I-95, sometimes called the Blue Steel Highway, for sale to gangs from Brooklyn, New York to Toronto, Canada.

Americans are not distressed about the murder rates of their neighbours to both the north and the south, hugely impacted by the illegal overflow from scofflaw gun shops and hundreds of gun shows that Bureau of Alcohol, Tobacco, Firearms and Explosives (ATF) agents are discouraged from attending. In Mexico, thousands take to the streets to protest gang killings of Brazilian proportions. By contrast, what does Canada have to complain about? Its largest city, Toronto, has a murder rate of two per one hundred thousand, miniscule compared with the forty-six per one hundred thousand rate of Baltimore. Yet, more than half of those murders are committed with handguns easily purchased in the United States for smuggling across "the longest undefended border in the world."

It has been said that guns flow from areas of fewer restrictions into areas of greater restriction. A precipitous increase in the number of civilians owning or selling handguns in the United States inevitably affects America's neighbours. Canadians are fighting alongside Americans in Afghanistan as part of the NATO coalition and the War on Terror, but surely crimes committed on Canadian streets with smuggled paramilitary firing power amount to domestic terrorism. Most of the one hundred thousand Americans victimized by guns each year come from impoverished areas. Does that fact explain why their loss and infirmity are not treated as an epidemic of violence, as the Centers for Disease Control and Prevention insists? Or are those doctors in Atlanta just a bunch of bleeding-heart liberals?

It is sadly ironic that Justice Clarence Thomas, an African-American, tipped the balance in the five to four court decision, when so many victims of gun violence share his ancestry. While justice should transcend a judge's background, justice should not be blind to obvious human suffering.

Canada's aboriginal people have a disproportionate rate of incarceration, which approximates the high rate for African-Americans in the United States. However, it is the slaying of Caucasian Canadians downtown, rather than of darker-skinned Canadians in disadvantaged areas, that intensifies media coverage of street crime. Rates of overall crime have been declining. Nonetheless, Stephen Harper's Conservatives adopted ill-advised, Republican-style policies, such as mandatory minimum sentences that make prisons even more overcrowded, regressive and soul-killing places. Punitive laws against violence, without generous programs for easing poverty, improving childhood development and enforcing strict gun control, do little to lower the violent crime rate. Witness the United States. It has the second highest incarceration rate in the world, after Russia, without having stemmed its epidemic of gun violence. If warehousing minorities in privatized prisons actually controlled crime, the United States would be safer, by now, than Scandinavia.

Canada has but one handgun manufacturer, Para-Ordnance, which operates in Scarborough, Ontario, a suburb of Toronto. Without shame or remorse, it aggressively markets its slick pistols to American civilians. In my view, this business should be taken over by the federal government, or, at the very least, restricted to selling its weapons to men and women in uniform. Canada cannot contribute to the growing problem of gun violence in the United States and then ask the American government to do more to block illegal guns crossing our border. While Canadians may still purchase handguns after intensive background checks, Toronto mayor David Miller has launched a movement for a national handgun ban. Also, both federal and provincial governments are being pressured to disallow gun collecting within city limits.

Unfortunately, as of summer 2008, the suburban 905 regions and commuter towns around Toronto also saw a steep increase in gun crimes. A not-in-my-backyard approach to ending gun collecting and club membership within city limits simply exports the problem nearby.

Ironically, by calling handgun ownership a right of self-defence, the American Supreme Court may have inadvertently set the stage for court challenges to *collecting* guns within civilian homes, given that just a single gun, a home-use taser or a large dog should offer even the wary homeowner a feeling of being protected.

Canada shares with the United States a vocal pro-gun lobby, euphemistically named Canadian Institute for Legislative Action (CILA). This organization frequently hosts speakers from the National Rifle Association, and engages its own members in letter-writing campaigns very similar to those in the United States, urging lawmakers not to blame 'the poor, inanimate gun' whenever another civilian gun death bloodies our streets.

I personally doubt that the first African-American president will stir up the hornets' nest of the wealthy, vociferous and heavily voting gun lobby. That more of the American public is not alarmed by ubiquitous firearms may be attributed to movies, television and hip hop music, which present guns as solving more problems than they cause. However, once in office, might President Obama remind the country that gun violence on the streets of American cities every year affects more than the combined casualties in the Iraq War over the past five years? In his nomination acceptance speech at the Democratic National Convention, Mr. Obama had the courage to say: "The reality of gun ownership may be different for hunters in rural Ohio than for those plagued by gang violence in Cleveland, but don't tell me we can't uphold the Second Amendment while keeping AK-47s out of the hands of criminals." Even this understated example was bound to ruffle feathers at the National Rifle Association, whose stand on any form of gun control is akin to "brook no quarter." In their "thin edge of the wedge" philosophy, today it's the AKs, tomorrow the handguns, and the day after, anything that fires a round.

American physicians must engage in further dialogue with one another and with physicians in neighbouring Canada and Mexico. We are all North Americans, supposedly "the three amigos." None of us wants to see the kind of explosion in gun violence now besetting Brazil become the new norm in North American cities.

There are more than fifty-three jurisdictions in the United States that can legislate on firearms policy. True change in this area is never easy and is always fraught with controversy. But a country where many people claim religious affiliation and hundreds of thousands are willing to march for "The Right to Life" can hardly overlook a combined death and injury count of one hundred thousand each year.

Clearly, there is something psychologically elemental behind the widespread emotional appeal of guns as an extension of the authentic masculine self. That alone could account for the gun lobby's success, as it urges its membership to ignore the statistics and risks, and hang on, at any cost, to something as precious as a part of their collective anatomy.

Part Two: Guns and Maleness

Got the raven two-five inside of my denim
Some said I was the child with the devil in him
– "Ghetto Bound" on the hip hop album *Free*, as quoted in *Enter the Babylon System*, by Rodrigo Bascunan and Christian Pearce.

By a close five to four decision, the affirming Court Justices went where no court has dared to go before. Chief Justice Antonin Scalia, no Founding Father but a father of nine, justified the decision to enshrine home gun rights in America by serving up a B-movie film image: a homeowner pointing a handgun to pin down a felon, while the other hand dials the police.

On January 9, 2009, the news services actually did report a case of an eighty-five-year-old granny in Pennsylvania who trained her gun on a seventeen-year-old intruder, getting him to call 911 and freezing him until the police arrived. The story is particularly newsworthy in that neither the granny nor the would-be burglar ended up dead. It was accompanied by news from New Jersey of an insurer lobbying for a new gun for seniors called The Palm Pistol which might be paid for by Medicare.

The NRA needs such unlikely stories, because on the very same day, there were also news reports of a four-year-old Ohio boy who shot his babysitter twice (charges, readers were assured, would not be laid) and of a twelve-year-old Arizona boy who shot his mother multiple times, causing her death. Later that same month, an eleven-year-old boy in Wampum, Pennsylvania fatally shot his father's pregnant girlfriend, using a "junior shotgun" he had been given for Christmas, with which he had earlier won a turkey shoot.

It was a tragic parody of the coming-of-age story of nine-year-old Ralphie, who persists in his wish for an air rifle as a Christmas gift, in the classic family film *A Christmas Story.*

The conservative judges on the Court donned their judicial blinders and effectively declared open season on sensible gun control law with the *District of Columbia v. Heller* Supreme Court decision. (My automatic ethno-political monitor reports that both Liberal Jewish judges voted against the decision, while the sole African-American judge, Clarence Thomas, helped make it a majority decision.) Their ruling extends to all American jurisdictions, even those such as Chicago, New York and San Francisco where largely successful handgun bans are now in place.

It is not in Justice Scalia's job description to acknowledge that, for many, guns are props in shoring up their sense of manhood. This is as true for wayward African-American or Latino kids from housing projects as for lonely white or Asian 'nerds' hunched over their first-person shooter video games. The need for a handgun is analogous to many American men's attraction to brawny SUVs and oversized pick-up trucks, although most macho European males are content to zip around in fast, sporty little vehicles.

Nor would the judges have much to say about Hollywood's glorification of guns, which provides such effective marketing for American gun manufacturers. The early seventies, a low point in American filmmaking, saw a spurt of movies where initially well-intentioned or liberal but learned heroes were mugged or threatened, until they finally picked up a gun and blasted away. These movies included *Straw Dogs, Death Wish* and the *Dirty Harry* series. The latter helped make the reputation of the Magnum, and the series was re-issued on video in 2008.

Nor were the justices interested in the gun fetishism of hip hop. These choice lines from the song "Terror Squadians," again as quoted in Canadian authors Bascunan and Pearce's groundbreaking book, meld gun worship with hostility to the all-powerful mother figure:

> I got rubies on my Uzis and gems on my MAC-10s
> Diamonds on my 9s, and golden bullets just to match 'em
> Platinum Magnums with silver clips, real begets
> Shit, I'm gonna milk this bitch 'til I'm filthy rich.

Much of gun fetishism among youth relates to paternal absence or to hostility towards an unreliable or abusive father. There are men on the streets built like Shaquille O'Neal or Sylvester Stallone who feel inwardly shaky about their male identity, recently having turned away from utter dependency on powerful moms and never having really known their dads. These men seem to need more than big muscles to feel unassailably male; they need props, like fast cars, expensive sportswear, pricey jewellery or, all too often, awesome firepower. Many of the conventional props that wealthier men rely on, such as secure jobs in positions of authority, are denied to kids from disadvantaged neighbourhoods by discrimination or lack of success in school programs that demand a considerable degree of conformity and early exposure to reading materials. Big men who feel small inside, who were slapped around or cowed into well-behaved submission as kids, may become walking time bombs of shame and rage as adults.

The long history of racism, addressed directly by Barack Obama in a bid to revive his briefly faltering Democratic leadership candidacy, may contribute towards a vehement support of gun rights in the southern United States. Many disadvantaged white males, in protest over the Civil War outcome, but also in fear of a freed, deeply abused and sexually mythologized slave population, form a fantasy alliance of good old boys to ensure that the white majority retains its psychological dominance and that others know their rightful place. Thus, in a given state, the higher the percentage of African-Americans, who mainly vote Democratic, the more likely the whites are to vote Republican, *en bloc.* In southern states such as Tennessee, where whites form a more solid majority, the vote tends to be more evenly split between Republicans and Democrats.

Buried even deeper than suppressed memories of brutalizing African slaves are memories of the genocidal expansion of the frontier that cost untold Aboriginal lives. The treachery involved had its parallels in Canada. Aboriginals were also displaced onto reservations, and successive governments ignored land claims, a wrong only recently beginning to be addressed. The residential school system imposed by zealous churches extended Canada's mistreatment of its First Nations peoples. The need for guns by the bedside has much to do with these deeply suppressed collective memories, all the stronger in those who harbour racism, whether consciously or unconsciously.

The adoration of guns and the frequently invoked "frontier mentality" was brought home when my wife's Uncle Dick pulled grandfather Waring's Civil War service revolver from the display case. His Uncle Drew's scrimshaw powder horn is of an even earlier vintage. A lot of people, especially Americans, have a fondness for historical firearms that are family keepsakes. When Charlton Heston made his "From my cold, dead hands" remark, he was referring, not to his hunting rifle, but to a Civil War antique he owned, thought to have belonged to General Robert E. Lee.

Mr. Heston ought to know that it's not *that* sort of gun that gun control advocates worry about. Rather, it is the rapid-fire Glocks, the cheap Saturday night specials and, of course, the AKs and Uzis on the streets of North American cities. As for middle-aged gun collectors who rush to purchase a spanking new semi-automatic pistol or rifle, simply because it 'starred' in a recent schoolyard massacre, well, that's another matter, though one psychologically related. Many of these men shore up their waning physical strength and sexual potency with what's in their display case. Even among the more stable collectors, there are many straight-ahead thinkers loath to apply wider moral considerations to what they view as a noble and innocent hobby.

The ubiquity of gun worship is part of why a "guy's flick" like *No Country for Old Men* could blow away the less macho competition and "violence was golden" at the 2008 Academy Awards. A Japanese joke describes the essence of popular movies as "Kissy-kissy, Bang-bang." That's not the order when the movie is American.

What made *No Country for Old Men* unusual was that its arch-villain Anton Chigurh, played by Oscar-winning Javier Bardem, took a pass on the sexy hardware featured in the film – such as the Tec-9 from the opening desert shoot-up, and even that handsome Desert Eagle revolver found and belted by the cowboy Llewelyn Moss, played by Josh Brolin. Instead, for much of the film, Chigurh preferred a hideous 12-gauge shotgun with silencer and a compressed-air, cattle-killing device that no gun collector in his right mind would covet, an instrument as devoid of sex appeal as the robot-like Chigurh himself. Nor did he have designs on Moss's lovely wife, with whom, like all his other helpless victims, he toyed after killing her husband. Like most serial killers, Chigurh was dead inside, and only violent power trips could arouse him.

After the tragic Virginia Tech shootings, many Americans reflected, however briefly, on how easily criminals or the mentally ill can obtain ruinously powerful firearms. The Second Amendment and the right to protect self and property are repeatedly invoked in defence of most firearms acquisitions by civilians. What few care to acknowledge is that guns are a quick and easy way for men to bolster their sense of masculinity, whether on the firing range or, more rarely, in urban society in a sport-hunting situation, but especially in a tough neighbourhood.

TASER International would love to horn in on, or at least indirectly benefit from, the lucrative gun market. A visit to its website reveals a Valentine's Day campaign called "Protect Her," whose aim is to put a "designer taser" in every bedroom of the nation. The newly minted C2 model comes in hot pink, *faux* leopard skin and camouflage patterns and fits nicely into a purse.

The men's men who peddle this "junk from the trunk" don't like to talk about someone like Cho Seung-Hui. This slight, extremely shy immigrant with an odd way of talking, repeatedly bullied as a "loser," found instant adequacy in the ability to take many human lives. In a better world, young men with shaky self-esteem might prove themselves by joining the police corps or the army, and march proudly alongside their fellow recruits. Not everyone, however, can meet the physical or psychological requirements of such jobs.

In such states as Virginia, nearly every man can walk the walk, and at one point historically, all citizens were obliged to own a gun and take formal training in its use.

Gun fanciers as a group like to think of themselves as "law-abiding good guys," immune to mental crack-ups. Yet both the Dawson College and Virginia Tech shooters started out as legal gun owners, who received training in the proper use of their weapons, as did the assassin of Northern Illinois University. In Toronto, a gunman settling a score outside a strip club accidentally shot the father of a nine-year-old who happened to walk past. The shooter had recently joined a gun club and had a legal right to carry his weapon through city streets.

It is eye-opening to visit some of the many gun makers' sites on the Internet. Start with Canada's very own gun manufacturer, Para-Ordnance. Note how enticing these handsomely cut guns are.

Most gun websites, such as Command Arms Accessories, appear starkly masculine in black and grey tones, will sell you an AK-47 where legal, or an Uzi or even a mini-Uzi and the kind of Glock or Walther pistols used by Cho to avenge his injured pride. Pink guns are not featured, not even for the discerning female shooter. As if to cover its tracks on the masculine protest issue, the gun lobby has come up with such fantastical creations as Pink Pistols, Gays and Lesbians for Individual Liberty and, my favourite, Jews for the Preservation of Firearms Ownership, whose meetings, I like to think, would probably fill a phone booth.

In 2006, in an address to the Canadian Shooting Sports Association (CSSA), National Rifle Association (NRA) President Sandy Froman said, "Ultimately, all guns are the same, and all gun owners are the same." To be fair, her preceding sentence was: "We cannot let our small differences divide us. We cannot let the anti-gun crowd turn hunters against pistol shooters, and gun collectors against trap shooters." She even quoted Benjamin Franklin: "We must all hang together or we will all hang separately."

Froman is a diminutive woman raised in the San Francisco Bay area, in a liberal family. She credits her conversion to avid gun ownership to a failed home invasion, when a man with a screwdriver tried to get into her apartment while she struggled, in vain, for her neighbours' attention as she anxiously awaited the police. She made a great deal of noise, and by the time the cops arrived, the man had fled, but she resolved never again to depend on law enforcement for her personal safety. Froman's solution to this potential home invasion might have been different had she read former police officer Frederic Storaska's book, *How to Say No to a Rapist and Survive.* Not one of his many creative suggestions involved a firearm, a weapon all too easy to turn on its holder.

Statistics on guns being turned against their owners or serving as magnets for burglars (guns are highly prized and easily fenced) don't deter the Sandy Fromans of the world. They certainly would not have deterred Kimveer Gill, the Dawson College shooter, who like Ms. Froman, legally obtained his firearms and the permits to use them. Nor would Ms. Froman have posed endlessly in the mirror, as did Robert De Niro's anti-hero in the film *Taxi Driver,* and Kimveer Gill and Cho Seung-Hui who loved brandishing their weapons in front of their webcams as much as they loved shopping for bullets and ammo clips on eBay.

Sandy Froman may have heralded a new generation of women, like John McCain's vice-presidential running mate, firebrand Alaska governor Sarah Palin, who adores hunting and fishing and is a card-carrying member of the NRA. It remains to be seen if this adamant pro-lifer recognizes the difference between devices that kill moose and those designed specifically to kill humans. Although she is pro-life rather than pro-choice on abortion, her position is the reverse on guns.

Lonely, estranged gun collectors do not represent the mainstream Joes who collect working firearms, but they are all smitten by the "stopping power" of their arsenals. (Gun websites love to boast about the "stopping power" of their products, but words like "kill" are avoided. Several sites offer a variety of "gun porn" links that sell not just leather holsters, but leather lingerie, sometimes featuring a woman in a see-through outfit, whose approving glance says, "What a man!") Self-styled heroes like Cho and Gill fantasize about triumphs on a dream battlefield to compensate for lack of success in fickle, rejection-prone dating.

Many teenagers today are hooked on first-person shooter (FPS) games and a mind-numbing array of violent video games, but *unlike* the ray guns in outer space battle movies, many of the weapons have real-life counterparts being heavily marketed "for police, military *and* civilian use." In FPS games, the extra points awarded for "headers" may help explain why the assassin at Northern Illinois University aimed for the heads of his fellow students. He, by the way, was one of the more socialized 'good guys,' a good-looking young man with a real-life girlfriend, who, by all accounts, studied and even taught criminology well. However, like many interested in such matters, he had a troubled past, in addition to an AK assault weapon and three handguns.

In a better world, people-killing guns would resemble the one made of flesh that shot human teeth in Canadian director David Cronenberg's film *eXistenZ,* instead of having slide-in, nickel-plated, extended-use ammo clips that easily elevate body counts. Truth in advertising would turn the motto of Para-Ordnance into "We make fine guns *and* paraplegics." Their precision-tooled pistols would be stamped with a big red and white, unsexy Canadian flag. (On its international website, Para doesn't mention being located in un-macho Canada.) In 2004, employees of the firm were implicated in a trafficking ring after unmarked handguns showed up on Toronto streets made with parts stolen from the factory. At the time of the trial, a detective testified that hundreds of Para-Ordnance handguns had been found at crime scenes in Ontario, fully half without serial numbers. The scandal gave the government an ideal opportunity to close down Canada's only handgun maker, yet today Para continues to sell to civilians in gun-infested countries such as the United States, Brazil and Algeria.

Working-class men, particularly those who are retired, layed off or unemployed, may view guns as a great equalizer, garnering respect from those who might otherwise devalue them. A gunrack and a bumper sticker on the back of a beat-up pickup truck reading "I'm the NRA and I vote" will slow down those who would cut off such a vehicle, as two smart-ass hippies on a fancy stretch motorcycle found out in the last scene of the iconic 1969 movie, *Easy Rider*.

Guns reinforce many men's sense of male adequacy. More puritanical than most European nations, the United States has a hard time admitting that widespread gun use is popular as an outlet for *both* sexual expression and sexual frustration. Many straight-edge kids hesitant about dating, masturbating or using substances are perfectly at ease endlessly fiddling with the paramilitary hardware provided on their personalized software. Many are eager to fiddle with the real thing and are hopefully more ready than the Massachusetts eight-year-old who accidentally shot himself to death with an Uzi at a firing range while his parents looked on in horror.

Might mature adult men who scoff at owning replicas or disabled weapons, and insist that the guns in their collection all be in perfect working order, accept some kind of compromise? In December 2008, Toronto gun owners traded nearly two thousand guns and sixty thousand rounds of ammunition for digital cameras offered by a local camera shop, in a police program called Pixels for Pistols.

I can envision a future hands-on Museum of the Contemporary Handgun, with hundreds of state-of-the-art models displayed alongside cheap Saturday night specials. Every weapon in the collection could be taken out and fired on designated ranges by those with the appropriate licences, all under tight supervision. Such a building belongs kitty-corner to the current Canadian War Museum located on the banks of the Ottawa River.

The current alternative is for society to keep placing its trust in a most unregulated 'militia' of amateurs scattered across North America, leaving them to their private devices, in the vain hope they don't give, lend or sell their guns to the wrong people or lose them to those who have designs on their unlocked safes or display cases.

Perhaps in the United States, concern over the gun burglary scene seems immaterial, when any disturbed individual can visit a scofflaw gun shop or gun fair. After all, there is extra money in selling to underworld types – and lots more macho points to be scored when you tell your wife about the heavy-looking dude who walked into your gun shop and ordered *twenty* of your best people stoppers, no questions asked.

There will always be men who are driven to commit evil acts. We pretend that we can protect ourselves and our families, should one or more of those men decide to pay us a call. Yet democratic society has institutions meant to protect its citizens. We should not maintain the fantasy of absolute self-protection when it endangers our families, our neighbours and innocent surprise visitors, like our teenaged daughter's boyfriend. Nor should we deny that the NRA gun lobby has encouraged gun companies and gun outlets to up the ante of lethality well past the point of sustainability.

Recently, a former attorney for the NRA, Richard Feldman, wrote an exposé on the organization, called *Ricochet: Confessions of a Gun Lobbyist.* While he remains a Second Amendment defender, the book, according to Mr. Feldman's publicity arm, MLS Communications, "unmasks the inner workings, influence and goals of this highly secretive political behemoth. From internecine warfare, media manipulation and executive bankrolling to gun control bills and school massacres, Richard Feldman, former NRA regional political director and lobbyist for the firearms industry, exposes the NRA as a cynical, mercenary political cult obsessed with wielding power while exploiting members' fear in order to maximize contributions."

One of the fruits of the NRA is its members' determination to subvert whatever legislation governments might pass. Here is what one of the thoughtful gun owners that I correspond with shared with me that points to just what gun control advocates are up against:

> Ron, an example that might interest you was the recent demise of federal legislation limiting the magazine capacity of certain pistols and rifles. Since banning high capacity magazines in existence prior to the legislation would have required an unenforceable attempt to remove private property (you know how the US loves private property) and compensate owners for this

> removal, the legislation specified magazines manufactured prior to the legislative date as exempt. Since magazines are very easily mass-produced using plastics, piano wire springs and metal stampings, some manufacturers figured that they would mass-produce, and I do mean mass-produce, millions of large capacity magazines prior to the enactment date of the legislation, the supply of which would last beyond the renewal or cancellation date of the law. It did and provided an enhanced source of income from those who felt deprived of high capacity magazines. The legislation was not renewed because American citizens have developed a finely honed way of side-stepping unpalatable laws, prohibition being one of them.

My training in child psychiatry brings me back to that school board in Harrold, Texas, which is encouraging teachers to be armed during classroom sessions, ostensibly to prevent another Columbine from happening. This grotesque distortion of the teacher-student relationship sets a terrible example of how those in authority comport themselves in the world. If the kids' fathers didn't have guns at home, they would be infinitely less of a potential threat to their teachers.

One last time, I dip into the deep well of Bascunan and Pearce's book for a quote by "man's man" Sean Connery. In an ad played in thousands of UK theatres, advocating the coming, successful ban on handguns, he stated: "It is said that a total ban on handguns, including .22s, would take away innocent pleasure from thousands of people. Is that more or less pleasure than watching your child grow up?"

Pop, Pop, Pop: The Sound of Violence

Americans seem unwilling to recognize that the country's lack of adequate gun control has reached truly epidemic proportions under George Bush.
(*The Toronto Star,* April 18, 2007)

How should Americans respond to the Virginia Tech slayings, the worst civilian massacre on American soil in modern times?

Pop, pop, pop went the usual banal sounds of unspeakable violence. Thirty-two people killed, at least fifteen more wounded. Afterwards, the gunman shot himself.

Yet, the usual, knee-jerk responses by President George Bush and the American news media are woefully inadequate.

Before the victims could even be identified, White House press secretary Dana Perino announced, after assuring citizens that "our thoughts and prayers are with the families," that "the president believes that there is a right for people to bear arms, but that all laws must be followed."

There you have it. The National Rifle Association must be appeased from the outset. Let's not start blaming assault weapons and semi-automatic pistols.

A second woeful response came from CNN's Paula Zahn, who, in commenting on the school's failure to notify students of the first shooting an hour or more before the second shooting, remarked that the school may be facing some serious liability in this matter.

There it is again. This is all that Americans can come up with, in answer to the gun tragedies that repeatedly ravage their land. They can offer prayers, they can wonder, "Why oh why would anyone do such a thing?" and they can initiate lawsuits, of anyone other than the makers of the very firearms used to take the lives of their children.

They are unable or unwilling to recognize that the country's lack of adequate gun control policies have reached truly epidemic proportions under the two consecutive terms of George Bush.

The Senate and House of Representatives, while still under Republican control, delivered two special gifts to the NRA, which is as adamant about protecting citizen rights to owning Sturm, Ruger assault rifles or Beretta pistols as it is to their owning hunting rifles.

The first gift was from then Republican House leader Tom DeLay, who allowed a "sunset clause" to end a bill that banned civilian ownership of various assault rifles. This bit of negligence occurred right in the middle of one of the most contentious presidential elections in American history.

The second gift, spearheaded through the Senate by then-Republican Senate leader Bill Frist, made gun manufacturers immune to lawsuits by those who are injured by their products, a bill similar to that of a law passed while George W. Bush was governor of Texas. His state also had no minimum age limit for the possession of a firearm.

Both DeLay and Frist were shifted from power due to their shifty campaigning practices, but their laws live on and continue to cause damage and to pile insult onto injury of those civilians who are massacred by some of the estimated two hundred and fifty million weapons in the hands of American civilians.

As Canadians, we have to be wary about human lives being made subservient to the interests of the gun lobby and the firearms manufacturers who so generously support that lobby.

Every massacre that occurs south of our border reopens the pain of our own L'École Polytechnique, Dawson College, Tabor, Mayerthorpe ...

In each case, civilians, usually unstable young men, were armed with paramilitary weapons that grotesquely increased their ability to harm others.

The very pop, pop, pop sound that is always described by witnesses of massacres these days – that is, the automaticity of weapons pouring off the assembly lines of gun makers – only swells the body counts of such tragedies and the likelihood of crossfire injuries whenever any kind of gun crime is committed. But then, a car marketed to Americans for years actually bore the name Pontiac Crossfire ...

Men like Prime Minister Stephen Harper or Public Safety Minister Stockwell Day know that those who collect working guns for a hobby or attend firing ranges tend to disproportionately support right-wing parties. What has yet to dawn on either man is that securing our schoolyards, the lives of our students and teachers is very much a part of "homeland security."

Indeed, our very political process is threatened by this over-proliferation of firearms in civilian hands, as was recently made clear when a career hit man admitted that a plan to assassinate former Prime Minister Pierre Elliott Trudeau was aborted only at the last moment.

Fully a quarter of all American presidents were either killed, wounded or shot at during their terms in office, according to a report in this month's *Medical Post.*

"If only some of those Virginia Tech students had been armed," cry the gun enthusiasts. Yet, our schools, colleges and universities should not have to turn into armed camps in order for young people to feel safe. Instead of introducing arms into our schools, we need to disarm the neighbourhoods around them.

As a psychiatrist, I deplore the naive belief the Americans have that more, rather than fewer, guns are what make us safer. It is part of a cynical doublespeak that contributes to a laxity about weapons control domestically and internationally.

It is this thinking that has led Prime Minister Harper to invest some seven hundred million dollars of taxpayers' money to arm and train our border guards, even though there have not been any shootouts at our borders, and even though border crossings would be the worst place for such shootouts to ever take place.

Despite the siren call of violence in TV shows and movies like *24, The Departed* and *The Sopranos,* and any other number of violent American confections, there is nothing sexy or wonderful about what happens to the lives of real human beings and their families once that banal but horrific, lethal pop, pop, pop sound defiles yet another public space.

The Trouble with Tasers

How rare, to be a trauma surgeon who moonlights on a Chicago Police Force SWAT Team! Yet, Dr. Andrew Dennis is just such a man. He and a fellow researcher recently cast a pall over the safety of taser guns. Their team zapped pigs with two forty-second taser jolts, then studied the effects on heart muscle function. They found that two sequential taser jolts could flip hearts into arrhythmia, especially when the barbed darts crossed the pig's heart – and even as late as three minutes after the initial jolt. Their findings bolstered those of a previous Toronto study, casting doubt on TASER International's claim that its product "has a better safety profile than Tylenol."

Mr. Tom Smith, co-founder with brother Rick of TASER International of Scottsdale, Arizona, briefed a Canadian parliamentary committee investigating the safety of the one-size-fits-all, fifty thousand-volt stun gun. Of the three hundred people in North America who died after being electrically incapacitated, TASER International claimed, only thirty suffered deaths to which the device may have contributed. Taser blamed even those deaths on co-existing factors, such as "excited delirium," a condition thought to be rare and not associated with intentionally criminal behaviour.

Canada-wide, seven thousand police officers rely on stun gun technology. Most of them believe TASER's safety claims, although a growing number have been injured during training sessions where they were on the receiving end of the excruciating device. While police chiefs have favoured proposals to ban civilian handguns, they are reluctant to remove an effective, if overused weapon from their armamentarium.

Why wouldn't gun fanciers want the lethality of tasers sorted out? For one thing, there is a lively debate about whether the taser should be classified as a "prohibited weapon" or a "prohibited firearm," and the distinction affects judgments on the legality of police forces to procure and employ the device.

The taser was first developed by NASA researcher Jack Cover in 1969. Initially, the device was propelled by gunpowder, and so the early version was classified as a firearm by the American Bureau of Alcohol, Tobacco and Firearms. The name "TASER" was an acronym for a fictitious weapon, "Thomas A. Swift's Electric Rifle." TASER International founder Rick Smith claims he decided to produce a "safer force option" after a "guy with a legally licensed gun who lost his temper" fatally shot two of his high school buddies. That fact alone might have given pause to advocates of firearms proliferation, who so often divide the world between the good guys who are legal gun owners and the criminal element who either purchase or steal illegal guns.

At their Scottsdale headquarters, the Smith brothers began work on a "non-firearm TASER electronic control device or ECD." The result was an "ergonomically handgun-shaped device using patented neuromuscular incapacitation technology, or NMI, that affected the recipient's sensory and motor nerves simultaneously, causing him or her to fall to the ground."

Tasers came under increased scrutiny following national coverage of the death of Polish immigrant Robert Dziekanski on October 14, 2007, after five taser jolts by one of four Royal Canadian Mounted Police (RCMP) officers trying to contain his increasingly erratic behaviour. The haste with which the taser was used, within eleven seconds of the officers' appearance, and the fact that the incident was filmed by another airport passenger, made the entire sequence of events notorious. Moreover, there was the unfairness: Mr. Dziekanski had been detained for many hours in an immigration holding area, and was not offered an interpreter, a bottle of water, a cigarette or anything else that might have helped calm him in the presence of large uniformed officers whom he recognized as police. In addition, that Mr. Dziekanki's Polish mother, an ideal interpreter, had been sent home rather than properly informed by airport officials of her son's whereabouts, made the incident even more excruciatingly unfair, as did the fact that the sleep- and nicotine-deprived Mr. Dziekanski had never before flown on an airplane. Here was an incident where having the available technology to subdue someone in short order trumped more humanitarian, if more painstaking options.

Once he hit the ground, Mr. Dziekanski was pinned by two of the burly officers, opening a subsequent debate about whether the taser jolts or something akin to "positional asphyxia" truly did him in. What no one can doubt is that Mr. Dziekanski was afforded minimum patience and humane consideration. Earlier, he had thrown a piece of airport machinery onto the floor, a cardinal sin in our technology-worshipping society.

In an equally dramatic, gut-wrenching situation in October 2008, mentally ill New Yorker Iman Morales was tasered while naked on the ledge of an apartment building, resulting in his falling to his death. Two days later, the distraught twenty-one-year veteran of the New York Police Department who had delivered the taser jolt against procedural guidelines, shot himself in the head rather than face the shame to himself and his family. Here again is a sequence in which both taser and handgun served as false solutions to humanitarian crises, with equally tragic results.

Several reviews of American police practices have pointed to likely overuse of tasers, not just to subdue dangerous felons, but to force immediate compliance with a variety of police orders. Typically, the taser is used in a direct-contact "drive stun" mode that does not fire projectiles, but elicits "pain compliance." The fact that tasers are carried by police officers even in the elementary schools of a few American cities raises particular concerns about their safe use and documented overuse.

The results of the RCMP investigation into the force's use of tasers were dragged into the open by *The Toronto Star's* request for access to information. In a rare moment in Canadian editorial history, the more right-wing *National Post* newspaper praised *The Toronto Star's* action, and called for the RCMP to exercise more transparency in the matter. The editorial "Safe Zapping" made additional demands: further studies into the safety of tasers conducted by independent investigators with no ties to TASER International; until the results of such studies proved conclusive, restriction of tasers and other CEDs to more experienced officers; and more restrictive guidelines for appropriate use, especially in such situations as Mr. Dziekanski's, when a victim is either on the floor or in handcuffs.

In a subsequent letter to the *National Post,* vice-president of the Canadian Association of Police Chiefs, T. J. Kaye, defended TASER International's sponsorship of his organization's annual meeting, and reiterated the police chiefs' commitment to the safety of the Canadian public. Particularly interesting about this group is that they have been clear advocates for a national handgun ban in Canada. Arguably, because of this stance, they are no longer represented on the Conservative government's Firearms Advisory Committee, heavily stacked in favour of advocates and apologists for the legal civilian possession of handguns.

It was not Police Chief Kaye's role to comment on TASER International's current aggressive marketing of sleekly designed CED products for civilian home use, such as the TASER C2 model now advertised on national infomercials in the United States. The commercials feature a pretty young woman incapacitating an Ultimate Fighting Champion. As I wrote to *The National Post,* the new models, designed to fit easily into a purse, come in a variety of colours, including "black pearl, desert camo, forest camo, leopard, fashion pink, red hot, electronic blue, metallic blue or titanium." One can even get a special Valentine's Day deal, as part of TASER's "Protect Her" campaign, or purchase a model that includes an MP3 player. At the October 2008 Consumer Electronics Show in Las Vegas, the sleek CEDs were displayed under the slogan "fashion with a bite." It is entirely legal both to own and carry such lethal fashion accessories in some forty-three states in America as well as in some European countries.

TASER International's arguably irresponsible, purely profit-driven behaviour echoes California's "Ring of Fire" handgun makers. Their goal is to supply as many lethal units to anyone who seeks self-protection, at low cost and regardless of the dangers to both their owners and their families, especially children. That the C2 looks as enticing as a toy seems no problem to its manufacturers. Similarly, Lauer Custom Weaponry based in Wisconsin sells a rich palette of gun paint products, each of which renders a real handgun or rifle indistinguishable from a plastic toy gun. When New York City mayor Michael Bloomberg banned the use of such paint in the State of New York, the company renamed its new line of designer colours The Bloomberg Collection EZ Camo Kit. Interviewed on CNN, the daughter of the company founder claimed that she was not personally concerned about safety hazards. Each threat had to be evaluated by law enforcement, including that of a child or adolescent pointing a plastic or real gun at another child, let alone at a police officer. She seemed blithely indifferent on the matter.

It is appropriate that gun-crime-ridden cities such as Milwaukee, Cleveland, Chicago and Toronto are casting a wary eye at TASER International. The company is accused of cherry-picking scientific studies that exonerate its products and is known to use aggressive lawsuits to intimidate researchers, journalists and coroners critical of its powerful products. Some are less than sanguine about any device that delivers a dose big enough to subdue a Rodney King to your average seventy-kilogram male, let alone a lighter weight female. The trouble with tasers is the trouble with handguns, on a reduced scale. Their sheer proliferation contributes to a civilian arms race, which in turn reinforces the alienation of atomized individuals from their fellow men.

I gained a different perspective on the police misuse of tasers when I spoke privately with a career veteran of the Metro Toronto Police force, whom I will call Sergeant Deegan. Well over six feet tall, with an imposing build, Deegan claimed that when he first signed up with the police, it was expected that every now and then an officer would be involved in a physical scuffle, and might well receive some minor injury, such as a shiner or a broken jaw. Nowadays, Deegan continued, the entry of women and small-build minority groups into the police force, while it has its advantages, has reduced the physical intimidation needed for making arrests or controlling crowds. To compensate, police threaten to use their fancy gadgets. Deegan also agreed that the ubiquity of the new semi-automatic handguns makes officers less willing to risk a suspect, let alone a felon, accessing a weapon. When I asked if he thought the new semis were easier to fire, thus making for more trigger-happy officers, he thought they were, indeed. In the olden days, said Deegan, you had a small, set number of rounds in your gun and on your belt. The new, easy slide-in ammunition clips make for much more generous firepower.

Remember Chris Rock's joke, that criminals would be much more careful about how many rounds they fired if bullets cost way more than guns? They would be especially wary about carelessly spraying bullets at an intended victim.

While tasers may play a valuable role in select situations, there are studies that show their widespread use does not necessarily reduce the number of shootings by officers. Too often they are used to obtain instant compliance from unarmed, relatively unthreatening but authority-challenging or even mentally confused individuals. If their use generates widespread fear, of the "Don't tase me, bro" variety, it could motivate already angry youth to carry weapons themselves. Indeed, given the recent proliferation of tasers in the United States, your risk of being tasered by police may soon be exceeded by your risk of being zapped by a civilian!

Afterword

Soon after I wrote this essay the Canadian Broadcasting Corporation/ Radio Canada announced the findings of the largest independent study ever conducted on taser devices in a CBC News feature called "The Taser Test." Pierre Savard, an electrical conduction expert at L'École Polytechnique de Montréal headed the study, whose findings were validated by other scientists at both the Toronto General Hospital and Duke University. National Technical Systems, whose headquarters are at UCLA, also took part in the study.

No less than forty-four of the X26 models most widely used by North American police forces were methodically tested for their electrical output. This is significant, as a previous study done in Australia on taser output, widely circulated to police agencies, had involved the testing of but a single taser device. The CEDs in the Canadian study were randomly selected from a number of police forces across the US and Canada. Savard was shocked by his findings. Fully 10% of the units manufactured before 2005 were defective. A few simply did not work at all. Most concerning was that others delivered up to 50% more power than the maximum output that TASER claimed possible. Savard concluded that, in specific incidents where the tasers produced cardiac arrhythmia, these unexpectedly high outputs could be as much as 50% more likely to produce cardiac arrest, especially when the darts landed near the heart of their victim.

TASER was quick to dismiss these results, and restate their claim that their product is and remains by far the safest police option, but the RCMP, embarrassed by their own laxity about regularly testing the force's tasers, set up a protocol for testing more of their taser units produced before 2005.

L'École Polytechnique is, of course, the site of the worst gun tragedy in Canadian history, the site of the massacre of fourteen female engineering students by Marc Lepine. The CBC therefore wisely chose to involve American companies and American police forces in their study. Unlike studies sponsored by TASER International, the science was as clean as the driven snow, and can only send a chill through TASER's Scottsdale, Arizona, headquarters.

Further corroboration soon followed, with a UCSF study published in January, 2009, by Tseng et. al. in *The American Journal of Cardiology.* The researchers reviewed data from fifty American cities, and found a six-fold increase in sudden deaths during the year after police departments began deploying tasers, *without* any reduction in firearms-related injury or any decrease in physical injury to officers involved in making arrests.

Closer to home, the mother of Robert Bagnell, a man who had died after being tasered by police when he refused to leave his bathroom, said this, "This is Canada and that's the way we work. We're a caring people. If a weapon's not working, they have to either fix it or get rid of it." It's a sentiment shared by her partner in grief, the mother of Robert Dziekanski, and anyone else facing the prospect of being on the receiving end of a taser.

Guns, Lethality and the Big Lie

The world keeps producing more guns and bombs.
Isn't that where our problems begin?
(*The Toronto Star*, July 31, 2005)

After this year's Live 8 concert for the developing world, staged under the utopian motto "Make Poverty History," many hard-nosed realists poured water on the event's idealism, insisting that the 'real' problem in Africa is not a lack of awareness by the world at large but, rather, government corruption that prevents aid money from reaching the people who need it most. These realists insist that what these countries need in order to obtain peace and prosperity is democracy and decent infrastructure.

Neither the realists nor the utopians pointed the finger at the superabundance of weapons available to the scores of fanatical men who are at the heart of the continent's many conflicts, not to mention those of the rest of the planet. This is in spite of the fact that a UN-commissioned study reported this month that small-arms fire kills as many as three times more people than previously thought. The study found that worldwide deaths from pistols, rifles, machine guns, mortars and hand-held rocket launchers likely approached five hundred thousand people, three hundred thousand in armed conflict and another two hundred thousand in non-conflict situations. It is thought that women and children make up 80% of the victims. Over the past decade, an estimated two million children have been killed and some six million psychologically damaged, seriously injured or permanently disabled by some of the estimated five hundred million small arms in circulation at the time of the 2005 report.

The word "lethal" is derived from the Latin for death, but also from the Greek mythic Lethe, which, in Hades, was the river of forgetfulness. Those who drank of its waters completely forgot the past. The concept of lethality, used to evoke total obliteration and the embracing of that which is lethal, is missing from discussions about what is happening in the world's growing number of failed states and war-torn countries. Weapons manufacturers in the United States, Eastern and Western Europe, Russia and China have made the world a far more lethal place than ever before in its history. As a direct result, a variety of long-standing conflicts once localized in the developing world now threaten the most cherished institutions of the developed world: democracy, public safety, mass transit and financial markets.

Lethality is a concept unhampered by the pie-in-the-sky ring of terms like global disarmament. Politically neutral, it follows from common sense. The world has periodically been made aware of lethality, and thousands of lives have been saved as a result. In the 1960s, Ralph Nader exposed flaws in the design of automobiles like the Corvair and the Pinto that were putting people's lives at risk. More recently, a focus on the dangers of passive smoking and on the reckless use of taser stun guns have opened up new avenues for saving human lives.

Paradoxically, the inherently lethal nature of weapons has made them immune to serious discussion about the extent to which they are manufactured and disseminated.

Introducing the concept of lethality on the world stage and using it to inform our foreign policies would make Canada clearer about its alliances with the US, NATO and Europe, and its role in world peace. Simply put, it is not just the legality of military ventures that is open to question, but also their potential lethality.

When we focus on lethality, we are less likely to fall under the sway of the Big Lie of militarism – the canard that it makes strategic sense to ship more and more arms to the 'good guys' of a region in conflict.

This logic was invoked in the past to justify the overthrow of a popular socialist leader in Iran, the subsequent propping up of the shah and the arming of Contras and death squads in Central and South America.

Those who pieced together the destined-to-fail Oslo Accord were thinking about peace, but not about lethality. They stipulated that the Israelis provide the Palestinian Authority with some forty thousand rifles. Through other means, the Palestinians illegally obtained some sixty thousand more. Most of those weapons came back to haunt the Israeli military and civilian population as part of Arafat's about-face known as the second intifada.

Currently, the Americans are in the process of arming some one hundred and seventy-five thousand Iraqi regulars. How little they have learned from their massive arming of such poorly contained figures as the shah, Saddam Hussein and, indeed, Osama bin Laden.

I am indebted to a fellow psychiatrist, an American suicidologist named Edwin Schneidman, for clarifying the difference between mere distress, of which there is plenty in the world, and lethality. In estimating suicidal risk, Schneidman advocated the use of a binary scale to evaluate both the distress of potential suicides and their degree of lethality.

An example he gave was that of a troubled teenager with a history of cutting her forearms, who had recently broken up with her boyfriend. Such a young woman rates very high on the distress scale but low on the lethality scale, as her cutting is not likely to result in death.

By contrast, he offered the example of a thrill-seeking sailor who occasionally played the deadly game of Russian roulette. Such a man may not be highly distressed but, nevertheless, is very lethal and at considerable risk of completed suicide.

The combination of high distress and high lethality should be avoided at all costs. Yet, this very combination is now threatening the world because of the wide availability of explosive agents and the willingness of more people to turn themselves and their vehicles into bombs. One has only to turn on the nightly news for footage of crowds of mostly unemployed young men in developing countries brandishing high-tech weaponry.

TV viewers have come to accept this as natural. Such acceptance is part of the Big Lie that no one in the West is willing to confront. The enormous build-up of conventional weapons by the United States, Europe, Russia and China, and the sale or gifting of these weapons to curry favour among the resource-rich developing world is a global tragedy, of which the wars in Iraq and Afghanistan are but recent manifestations. These wars reverberate back onto the local scene; as Britain's Home Office recently admitted, the war in Iraq is a key cause of young British Muslims turning towards radicalism. We have but to ask ourselves this question to expose the Big Lie: since Kalashnikov rifles and rocket-propelled grenades (RPGs) are de-stabilizing Iraq and Afghanistan, why isn't the United States reading the riot act to the Eastern European nations and China who keep flooding the world with such weapons?

The motivation is not there, because 1) America's love affair with guns makes it myopic on the subject of militarism; 2) wealthy industrialists who own defence stocks and security technology stocks would feel the pinch if America herself closed down firms that make handguns or assault weapons for distribution to civilian populations both at home and abroad and 3) many US legislators in both Houses of Parliament join the boards of defence contractors after they retire.

Similarly, in Europe, a firm like Norway's Dyno Industrier ASA would be financially hurt if it were obliged to scale back on the HMX and

RDX weapons-grade plastic explosives it manufactures in one hundred different varieties and sells in forty countries around the world. Tonnes of this same type of explosive went missing from the munitions stockpiles in Iraq, only to wind up in the hands of Zarqawi and other insurgents. These military-grade explosives turn cars and trucks into giant grenades that almost always result in double- or triple-digit casualties.

When I was a child growing up in Winnipeg, our family often drove over the Salter Bridge past two huge words spray-painted on the side of a large cold-storage building. The slogan struck me then as that of an idealistic kook: DISARM NOW. No doubt some readers will dub me a dreamer for suggesting that the first step on the road to peace is to scale back the production and distribution of conventional weapons and explosive agents.

Some will argue that it is all too easy to produce homemade explosives and that the closing of commercial explosives factories will serve no purpose. Yet, the July 21st bombing attempt on the London subway system failed because the bombers' homemade explosives failed to detonate.

As well, the home manufacture of explosives is a dangerous business, one that often leads to unintended explosions. The commonly used chemical cocktail TATP, made out of drain cleaner, bleach and acetone, has been nicknamed "Mother of Satan" for the number of bombmakers it has maimed.

This homemade explosive is highly unstable and sensitive to friction and heat, which is why it is increasingly being mixed with military-grade explosives. Still, should it prove necessary to make drain cleaner, bleach and acetone tightly controlled products in areas beset by bombings, most citizens would breathe a sigh of relief. At any rate, they depend on an infrastructure of conventional weapons to safeguard their painstaking activities.

The endless array of explosives out there might seem bewildering, but most explosive agents contain substances in common that are easy to chemically detect, such as nitrates. Repeatedly, concerned American scientists have pushed to have explosives manufacturers tag their lethal products with easily identifiable chemicals that would provide a source code for the factories that made them.

However, the industry has balked at this, citing the increased liability that could result from explosives detonating prematurely or being misused in some way. American explosives makers also point out, understandably, that the need to source-identify explosive agents would have to be applied to producers in Europe, Russia and China, as well.

Where are the whistle-blowers at all the plastic-based explosive factories around the world? Why do our newspapers not provide us a map of the communities that give tax breaks and homes to such industries? Where are the men and women of conscience who would shut down those plants for a day, or a week, if only out of respect for the maimed and the dead, if only to give their governments a chance to pause for thought?

If we cannot shut down, or at least slow down, these death mills, whose only purpose is to kill people, are we not as complicit as IBM exporting its punch cards to the Nazis to help them track their victims' identities and possessions?

The biggest lie of all is reserving the term "Weapons of Mass Destruction" for nuclear, biological and chemical weapons when small arms have been the principle weapons used in up to 90% of conflicts in the last decade.

Afterword

An article for *Financial Times* in 2007 cited a report by the Government Accountability Office (GAO), the oversight arm of Congress, which questioned the Pentagon's grasp on what happens to weapons and equipment supplied under the twenty billion dollar American program to train and equip Iraqi security forces.

The US supplied Iraqi soldiers and police with one hundred and eighty-five thousand AK-47 assault rifles and one hundred and seventy thousand pistols between 2003 and 2005. But the GAO report said that the Pentagon had lost track of one hundred and ten thousand rifles and eighty thousand pistols. It also said the defence department could not account for one hundred and thirty-five thousand pieces of body armour and one hundred and fifteen thousand helmets.

And so it goes ...

Love, Death and Old Men

A 'love affair with the world' turned violent; spare a thought for all who are smitten.
(*The Toronto Star*, February 12, 2006)

O my love, my wife! Death, that hath sucked the honey of thy breath, hath no power yet upon thy beauty. Thou art not conquered. –Shakespeare, *Romeo and Juliet*

La petite mort – French nickname for orgasm.

At first blush, love and death seem like polar opposites. Love is tied to an attachment to the people and things of this world, while death is the ultimate renunciation of those attachments.

Yet, everywhere we look the two are linked, and even confused with one another, especially by the young. It is not unusual to talk about being "smitten" with love, or about dying for the love of a country or a god. The symbol of love's own holiday, Valentine's Day, is an arrow piercing a blood-red heart.

This winter in Toronto, it is possible to gaze at the morbid wonders of the human body at the Ontario Science Centre, as graphically presented in Dr. Gunther von Hagens' plastinated cadavers from Body Worlds 2.

The exhibit includes many people who, while skinned and partially dissected, retain unsettlingly lively features such as lips, eyebrows and vividly gleaming eyeballs. Two of the dead are youths forever holding athletic poses, one on a skateboard and another precariously poised as a ballerina in pointe shoes. Von Hagens is not the first to use the bodies of younger people to his own ends, but he had the courtesy to wait until they died rather than send them to their deaths.

Another death-defying show took place last month at the Buddies in Bad Times Theatre. Two aging but ageless striptease artists, Kitty Neptune and Sasha Van Bon Bon, did a send-up of female sexual stereotypes from old movie classics, reviving the memories of femmes fatales in a lively burlesque revue called *Under the Mink*. The two older women shook their more seasoned booties and managed to eclipse the four younger, slimmer dancers they hired on as eye candy for the show.

It may seem like a stretch to go from von Hagens and his cadaver scandals to Sasha Van Bon Bon and her Scandelles, but the intimate dance between love and death is a feature not just of our entertainments but also of the daily news.

Would that it were only in a tragedy like *Romeo and Juliet* that youthful passions are transformed into murderous acts. A group of cartoons was all it took to stir the passions of huge numbers of Muslims around the world, some of whom expressed their outrage at those who had mocked their beloved Prophet by threatening to "behead those who insult Islam." As always, the invisible hand of older men is behind mass demonstrations that elevate passion above reason and abstract principles above actual human lives. The theme of Islamic youth being lured into self-sacrifice is echoed in the promise that each young suicide bomber will receive, as reward, the company of seventy-two beautiful virgins, bounty enough for a successful shahid who blows up his or her earthly body in the name of destroying The Infidel. The message to youth from the older male generation is clear: You may enjoy an abundance of sensual pleasure, but first comes the awesome self-sacrifice in God's name. It is an extrapolation of the near-sacrifice of his son Isaac by the God-fearing Abraham of the Old Testament.

In the Christian tradition, two winter martyrs, St. Valentine and St. Sebastian, shared a love of their fellow men that sent each to a violent death by order of an older male generation.

Valentine was a Christian priest who secretly conducted marriages against the decree of the Roman emperor, Claudius II, also known as 'Claudius the Cruel'. The emperor was having trouble recruiting young people for his unpopular war campaigns and cunningly decided to cancel all marriages and engagements in Rome as a disincentive to civilian life. Valentine helped out not only Christians but also other star-crossed Roman couples. Legend has it that before he was martyred (he was beaten and beheaded on February 14th), he left a note for his jailer's daughter reading, "From your Valentine."

Preceding Valentine's Day, on January 20th, is a feast honouring St. Sebastian, another young man, who enlisted in the Roman army with the secret intent of comforting Christians who were martyred. He showed such prowess on the battlefield that he was made a captain by

Emperor Diocletian, but as more and more Christians were put to the sword, Sebastian's sympathies were found out and he was condemned to be shot by archers. Despite many gruesome wounds, including an arrow to the heart, he was nursed back to health by the Christian, Irene. As soon as he could stand, Sebastian sought out Diocletian, not to beg for a reprieve but to accuse the Emperor of the many cruelties he had committed. For his boldness, Sebastian was subsequently beaten to death. Considered the patron saint of archers and soldiers, he should, in my view, be named the patron saint of conscientious objectors.

It is here that I would ask the reader to find a copy of Wordsworth's famous ode "Intimations of Immortality from Recollections of Early Childhood" and its epigraph poem, "My Heart Leaps Up". The poet asks what became of the beauty of a world he once saw through innocent eyes. Using immortal phrases like "splendour in the grass, and glory in the flower," and "the child is father to the man," Wordsworth asks why the imagination seems to shrink as we grow older. Why is true inspiration so hard to achieve in our adult years? How can one reclaim the "love affair with the world" of early childhood?

Wordsworth winds up accepting as consolation for the loss of innocence, his ability to enjoy precious aspects of the earthly world. However, he refuses to stop there and, for greater consolation, he chooses a full love of the world through rebirth after death. As with the resurrection theme, Wordsworth sees in death and the afterlife the fullest way to rejoin humanity and the Creator.

As Kurt Vonnegut might say, "And so it goes ..." There is no route to the fully realized life but through death. Wordsworth laments young people's desire to grow up too quickly, given the "visionary gleam" they lose in the process. It is only by the light of such early inspiration that humanity can grasp the "immortal sea" of eternity.

Yet, for too many young people, the passions of childhood get exchanged for the passions of war and the risk of early death. The emperors and the high priests among us corral young people into causes, crusades, and merciless quests for honour and revenge. The friendship of childhood is exchanged for the camaraderie of a military company, and the eroticism of youth gives way to the unbridled passion of all-out war. The young are promised glory, or even eternal life and love, but only after they undergo a life-affirming death. Think of it as a universal Catch-22.

We know the real enemies of youth from the impossible missions they set, the sacrificial altars they build, the weapons they freely disperse, the aluminum keys they issue to Heaven and from their seductive, often lecherous invitation to young people to use them as exclusive guides to the truth or to contact with the Divine. They are experts to a man at stirring youth into an orgasmic frenzy of hatred of a demonized other.

At a time when acts of consummate rage are committed in the name of love of God and country, the connection – or the confusion – between love and death is more compelling on the world's battlefields and terrorized civilian spaces than in its bedrooms.

These hard realities, which saw their climax in World War II and the Holocaust it spawned, drove a downcast Sigmund Freud, a deep believer in the life-giving power of the erotic instinct, to concede equal billing to what he named, with regret, the "death instinct."

May we contemplate both instincts this Valentine's Day as we draw an arrow through the human heart and think of all those youths who are smitten, whether with unrequited love or by pointlessly violent death.

Section Two

Health

"The Art of Psychiatry"

Letter to the Editor
(*The Globe and Mail,* November 2008)

Toronto – While your article is right to showcase the discrimination against psychiatry that exists even in the medical profession, it does not ask if there is something about the admissions criteria used by medical schools – which over-select for the highest possible grades, and weight the sciences far above the arts – that may contribute to fewer medical-student applicants for psychiatry residency positions ("Psychiatry: A specialty relegated to the basement" – November 25, 2008).

While psychiatric treatments are, in some ways, more humane than ever, psychotherapy has become increasingly manualized and highly focused on circumscribed diagnostic entities. This shrinks the purview of the practice of psychotherapy. Indeed, many psychiatry residents these days barely study psychodynamic psychotherapy and often bypass the experience of entering therapy themselves.

This discourages, or at least may fail to entice, those who are truly interested in medical humanities and the light that psychiatry can shed on human nature in the broader sense.

Can Lassie Afford to Get Medical Help?

(*The Medical Post,* September 2, 2002)

I once saw a cartoon that resonates for me as a psychiatrist. In the first panel, a young boy has fallen through the ice and cries out to his dog: "Lassie, get help!"

The second panel shows Lassie on her back on an analyst's couch, trying to express her feelings – hardly the kind of "getting help" her desperate master had in mind.

The cartoon is a tale of aborted triage, all too relevant to a public medicare system quaking on its foundations. Someone falls into a mess, sends a trusted ally for help, but flounders as the wrong help is offered – and to the wrong party to boot! Similar events, amusing only as cartoon parody, happen many times a day in this country, when families have an acute mental health crisis, especially the abrupt onset of a mental illness.

Sometimes the result is not witnessed and tragic. To a socially withdrawn suicide, there is no Lassie to send and there may not be a Lassie to fetch in an under-serviced area.

At other times, one from the helping professions – Dr. Laddie or Dr. Lassie – can be contacted or, if willing, summoned on a house call, and that physician either deals with the situation on the spot or triages the troubled person to a medical specialist. The choice of specialist will affect whether help is offered for the long term, only temporarily or amounts to little more than a trip from the frying pan into the fire.

Factors such as geography and the knowledge base of the first helper contacted play a crucial role. If you suffer family or psychiatric problems in Toronto, for example, unless homeless or one of the marginal poor, likely you will have access to at least an emergency room. You may even be one of the fortunate with a family doctor to call on. On the other hand, if you live outside Timmins, Ontario, the brute facts of unequally distributed medical resources will loom large.

To collapse in Toronto rather than Timmins may well figure in your access to specialized, that is, psychiatric, help. Even then, if you suffer from schizophrenia or a psychotic depression and are sent to someone who knows little about such medical conditions and nothing about emergency medications, you can be in as much trouble as the little boy in the cartoon. Alternatively, if you are being scapegoated and abused by family members and are sent to a psychiatrist who treats everything with pills, you may wind up doped, dusted off and returned to the firing line – only this time, with even lower credibility from a mislabel of psychiatric illness.

Last, consider a man depressed by an unsympathetic boss and financial problems, to whom a specialist offers three treatment sessions a week, at fifty dollars per session more than the provincial plan reimburses. Such "extra billing" is akin to Lassie biting her master's hand in the hope that he will jump out of the frozen river in rage. A person in crisis may not realize he or she is under neither legal nor moral obligation to pay the therapist any amount greater than that reimbursed by the provincial plan. While it is true some provincial plans pay specialists a puny hourly rate relative to that of their colleagues south of the border, such matters ought to be settled between the doctors and the province, not on the back of a person in crisis. Ought the boy to have cried out, "Lassie, get help – but keep it within our means!"?

A Post-Mortem on Body Worlds 2

Body Worlds 2, the anatomy extravaganza by the controversial German pathologist Dr. Gunther von Hagens, has come and gone, and, true to its advance billing as a sure money-maker, attracted nearly four hundred thousand visitors to The Ontario Science Centre. In a mild winter Torontonians saw ads for the show with arresting images of cadavers called *The Ponderer* and *The Skateboarder* on the walls of bus shelters and in the arts sections of the newspapers.

The anticipated criticism by community religious leaders was muted. There was a critical article in the *Canadian Jewish News* by the rabbi emeritus of Holy Blossom Temple, Dow Marmur, calling into question the ethics and sensibility of such a show, but generally, religious leaders backed down from any kind of group censure or from providing guidance as to how, or by whom, such a show should be viewed.

After all, the Body Worlds exhibits have garnered an audience of some seventeen million people in twenty-two countries around the world over the past ten years. If there were something fundamentally wrong about the shows, surely someone would be out picketing them? The venues would impose age restrictions on those who could attend. Or, in capitalist societies, is spectacular commercial success reason enough to celebrate shows like Body Worlds 2?

Perhaps it is time, in the clear light of spring, to do a post-mortem on the show, and speculate about possible after-effects on some of its youngest visitors. This was, after all, a show filled with the naked dead, a show in which genitals, breasts and buttocks, both whole and partially dissected, were much in evidence and viewed up close.

Admittedly, the Ontario Science Centre did do a nice job preparing the thousands of visitors whose curiosity or morbid fascination drew them to Body Worlds 2. The Centre website featured previews of colour photographs of several specimens of the plastinated bodies with which Dr. von Hagens tours the world. These included his artistic *The Ponderer,* a skinned, muscular male sitting on a hewn stump, after the manner of Rodin's *The Thinker*, his every muscle and bone available for inspection.

From the long lineup outside the exhibit, where I stood with my wife and adult son, one could preview some cadavers on closed-circuit television. Clearly, the principle was *caveat emptor*, even if the show was a celebration of von Hagens' mission statement: "I am here to democratize anatomy. You are here to see what the experts have *enjoyed* (emphasis mine) for centuries." In response to criticism around issues of informed consent, he had written, "This is not an illegal cemetery. It is a hall of enlightenment and when you learn you cannot mourn. The relatives come. They enjoy looking but they don't know who is who and that is justified." On a more profound note, he hung beautiful quotes from great thinkers like Epicurus of Greece and by the great Germans Kant and Goethe, with whom von Hagens is said to share a hometown.

Winding our way with other families small and large, a few with children in strollers, we inched past the glass cases of a long anteroom, viewing the least disturbing things first: individual bones of the human body, a disembodied finger, a hand with long fingernails, a dissected brain in slices and a spinal column with its hundreds of radiating nerves. Slowly we were being desensitized, before being released into an enormous exhibition space filled with well-preserved corpses in athletic poses, that to some, was a heaven of rational enlightenment.

As psychiatrist and poet, I had come to evaluate both von Hagens' science and his art, to ponder mortality in the midst of a large, supportive crowd, but also to gauge the reaction of the audience to such a revolutionary display. Long before Body Worlds 2 opened, I had written a letter to *The Globe and Mail* suggesting The Science Centre implement an age requirement for viewing such an exhibit, perhaps ten or twelve or fourteen years. The idea of children under the age of five viewing such an exhibit filled me with concern verging on dread.

There was relatively little text appended to these specimens that so clearly spoke with every sinew. *Res ipse loquitur* (The thing speaks for itself). Those descriptions that were provided, for example that which described *The Head Diver*, were dryly factual, in the fashion of a dispassionate anatomist: "The torso is frontally divided and both sides folded from each other, with the brain removed from the cranium and now found at the top of the spinal column." Here was a woman who had suffered more than a bellyflop. She was split down her very core and, were she somehow still alive, would have been relieved to realize her brain was still part of her.

In general, what struck me about the specimens was how the plastination process invented by von Hagens allowed them to maintain the same kind of delicate balancing act that he himself has to master, trying to present dead bodies as a kind of educational statuary far removed from their all-too-human original human owners. There was the young skateboarder, the muscles of his rear cut and pulled back in flaps; there was a body slinking head-first down a pole; a yoga woman; a javelin thrower and even two ice-skating dancers holding an eternally ravishing pose, with more kinetic grace than the benign Invisible Man/Woman series of anatomy figurines from my childhood, just a nose away from those respectfully gawking. There was even an enormous, skinned camel with a swathe of her fur still on and her young, also standing, also partially dissected, right next to her.

The more disturbing of the specimens, to my eye, were those with whose physical features von Hagens' had most tampered. The head of *The X-Lady* was so cruelly dissected that she resembled a giant insect, albeit with a human torso and her legs crossed in an X. She was horrific and surreal. Such a human specimen was more a tribute to what the anatomist's toolkit could achieve than to the human form. The same could be said for *The Drawer Man,* and the body parts of *The Exploded Body* which, hanging from a hundred or more transparent strings, brought to mind the image of a suicide bomber mid-detonation.

Most memorable of all was a small, slightly darkened room that invited the viewer to witness the wonders of human reproduction. Inside were several jarred embryos at various stages of gestation, and at the back, peering from behind a plexiglass case with dazed eyes, a woman who had died while still carrying a baby at five months, the back of her shoulder-blade cut away to reveal "a smoker's lung." Hers was the ultimate cautionary tale, and yet, there they were to behold, dead mother and her baby *in situ.*

As I exited, I did not recall seeing a single Orthodox religious Jew wearing yarmulke at the exhibit, and very few who looked of Muslim origins. When I spotted two men with a South Asian look, accompanied by their two young boys who looked about seven or eight, I approached them. "Pardon me, but were you in any way offended by this exhibit?" "Oh no," one of the fathers answered without hesitation. "We are Buddhist. For us, death is very much a part of life."

It reminded me that some people claim that von Hagens' shows inclined them to make positive lifestyle changes. Often cited are the exhibits of normal lungs alongside a smoker's lungs and a coal miner's lungs and the display of the effects of obesity on internal organs. I recalled that some restaurants use von Hagens' plastinating process in food displays, since it makes everything look more colourful and tastier.

Dr. Gunther von Hagens, who revolutionized the anatomy display, was, as a boy, in an intensive care unit himself, with a serious bleeding disorder. As an adult, he was imprisoned for two years by the East

Germans for anti-Communist views. Now a major curator, some would say a human anatomy impresario, his shows employ a team of dissection experts and he has made a fortune touring his unique cross between medical science and freak show across the world. The shows are especially popular in Asia, the source of many of his earliest cadavers.

This immersion of lay citizenry into the halls and ways of death might be something a doctor could applaud. Yet, centuries of laws against the desecration of corpses and trafficking in dead bodies for material gain do not vanish for an anatomy show, however popular. My inner physician would debate with my inner poet, indeed with my inner religious sense on the probity of what I had just seen, likely for many months. It seems that there are many experiences for which it is necessary to split off the intellectual from the emotional faculties in order to partake of the experience. Surgeons have to do this when they perform an operation on a living, breathing human being. To one trained in the healing arts, it is not that difficult to appreciate the wonders of a specimen like *Orthopedic Body,* a female cadaver whose body was fitted with every conceivable type of prosthetic appliance, from jaw implant to artificial hip and knee. Yet, even a trauma surgeon might choose to stay away from a "slice 'n dice" horror flick.

After I left Body Worlds 2, having bought a few postcards in the Science Centre gift shop, I felt exhilarated. Not only did I rediscover the engineering wonders of the human body, but had done so in a bustling public venue, alongside hundreds of fellow Torontonians, wondering how each was processing their individual encounters with our shared mortality. It was only later that I realized that I was feeling more overstimulated than exhilarated. It had all been a bit much, in the end, not just violating so many societal taboos, but also doing so with many fellow parents who made the dubious choice of bringing their little ones along for the ride. I had experienced the same pangs on hearing that many fundamentalist Christians chose to take young children to see the movie *The Passion of the Christ* by Mel Gibson, a man who shares von Hagens' fascination with the human body *in extremis.*

There may be young children who are immune to the darker side of such exhibits. I leave it to the reader to decide whether they are hearing in my misgivings more of the overly sensitive child I was than the psychiatrist concerned about avoiding unnecessarily traumatizing children that I have become.

I remember now what Rabbi Marmur said when I asked him, in person, what he had thought of Body Worlds 2: "It was like a walking tour of Hell." I later asked a physician friend of mine what he had thought. He pointed out there had been quite a debate around the issue of informed consent. “Who would agree to live on forever as *Drawer Man* or *X-Ray Lady?*” He continued, “It wasn’t really my thing.” He then shook his head. “This is going to sound wrong. but I can’t stop thinking, Leave it to the Germans ...”

Death at Arm's Length

(*The Medical Post,* June 1, 2004)

Not long ago, I stepped gingerly across the mid-century mark and now have as many misgivings about being a "ripe, old age" as I used to have about the possibility of not reaching a ripe, old age. As a young man destined to become a psychiatrist and poet, I was mindful of the possibility of an early death – one that might deny me my flickering statement here on Earth. I breathed easier once I outlasted, in sequence, Keats's twenty-five, Mozart's thirty-five and Robert Louis Stevenson's forty-four years.

As a young child, my vision of death was born of having been dragged along by my older brother and his friends to watch horror movies. It took the form of a long, bloodless arm reaching out to grab me from underneath the stairs, much like one of the images from the animated film *The Nightmare Before Christmas* by Tim Burton.

As children, my brother and I had a benign arm's-length relationship with the Great Nullifier, a fairly charmed relationship in fact. Our grandparents had died before we really got to know them and we had the good fortune of not losing anyone near to us until our late adolescence and early twenties. By then, we were well-armed with adolescent bravado and denial.

Our parents, of course, fared less well. Every week or two my mother would answer a particular kind of telephone call, which made her fall silent as someone on the other end broke the dreaded news. We knew it was unwelcome tidings because she would grow pale and say something like, "Oh, no." At that point, if in listening range, my brother and I would zero in, eager to solve the mystery. Did a younger male family acquaintance suffer a slipped disc, a heart attack or a stroke (whatever that meant), or was it simply another elderly family acquaintance who had shuffled off their mortal coil? Sometimes we innocently chimed in our best guesses: "Mr. Adelman? Mrs. Elkin?" – in the spirit of some kind of existential game of Jeopardy. By contrast, when our mother would read in the papers about some tragically early demise, she could usually shake its pall with the magic words “Nobody we know,” as if to say, “Not to worry, one more death at arm’s length.”

The loss of our beloved mother, and later our father, forever put an end to our arm’s-length relationship with death.

Beam me back to my fifties, and it is sometimes my turn to field those familiar old phone calls we dread. Sometimes they involve male acquaintances suffering heart attacks and strokes; more likely they concern men who must undergo emergency cardiac bypass procedures, or who have suddenly, unexpectedly, joined me as members in the bad-back club. The calls about women being diagnosed with breast or ovarian cancer are concerning in their frequency. These are more intimations of mortality than true death notices, cancer having been, for the most part, downgraded to a potentially disabling chronic illness with five-year and ten-or-more-year ‘survival rates.’

By this point I can almost hear my late mother shushing me, warning about the evil eye that attends anyone even mentioning death in anything but the gravest of tones. But even in my medical school years, while I was obliged to poke away at pickled cadavers in the dissecting room and attend the occasional autopsy, which truly was unsettling, I had the unusually good fortune of never witnessing a single person die before my eyes. This spoke to the skill and acumen of the surgeons and post-op nursing staff in the Winnipeg hospitals in which I took my pre-psychiatry training.

As a practising psychiatrist, I regularly address the fears my patients have of death and try to intervene in plans some have for putting an untimely end to their lives. While I have never had the misfortune of losing a patient in my care to a self-inflicted death, there have been close calls, and I can see my mother pointing to something made of wood for me to touch (preferably my head) for even making such a statement.

I have come to think of my own death in the same way I do about a personal god. Both are constant, if somewhat abstract, companions and both are quite simply beyond intellectual comprehension. Perhaps it is because I cannot understand them that I write about them, and only through the medium of poetry can I do so on what feels like sound footing. I invoke these abstract concepts in my daily life whenever I need comfort or perspective.

As I grow older, more people I cherish or depend upon will be taken from me and I find this brute fact more disturbing than contemplating my own demise. Only the death of a child or an untimely death of a defender of human rights fills me with a true sense of futility.

The best way to deal with a disabling disease is to use a healthy measure of denial and humour, which may be the best way to approach our own existential situation. This comes easily to the lucky ones – those who have been gifted, at least in their early years, with an arm's-length relationship with death – rather than those who have been ravaged by the early loss of loved ones. The use of denial, however, veers off into the unethical when applied to our society's engaging in policies that result in the deaths of others.

The other day I had the flippant thought, "Everyone always talks about death, but only men like bin Laden and George Bush actually do something about it." I dismissed this paraphrase of our existential weather as quickly as I did a limerick I wrote in medical school, inspired by a quirky pathologist I met who was unable to say the word "death" without breaking into a painful stammer. For this speech impediment, I substituted a lisp, an affliction known to affect no less esteemed and death-defying a forbear than the great emancipator Moses:

A Pathologist name of Macbeth
Was heard mumbling under his breath:
"Though my lithp may dithgrathe me
when live pathienths fathe me,
I can thtill very nithely thay:
Death."

Mythic Marijuana

In the winter of 2008, Canada's "Prince of Pot" Marc Emery nearly accepted a plea bargain. It would offer him a five-year jail term in a Canadian prison, rather than extradition and possible life imprisonment in the United States. His lawyers urged him to acquiesce to spare his co-accused, the other two of the "BC3," from incarceration. One of them was Michelle Rainey, who uses marijuana as a medical treatment for her Crohn's disease.

In the spring of 2008, the Conservative government of Stephen Harper reneged on the plea bargain. Emery and his two associates were charged in the United States and face sentences of ten years to life if convicted. The charges include money laundering. Ruling on a similar case, an appeal court judge suggested that a one-month jail sentence and probation would be adequate for the crime of selling marijuana seed if Marc Emery were charged in Canada. That ruling could be used to Emery's advantage in his fight against extradition.

The pro-marijuana lobby claims that the Americans are hounding the Vancouver exporter of millions of marijuana seeds across Canada and into parts of the United States partly because of his success as a soft-drug entrepreneur. Emery, who pays taxes on his business, described himself on tax forms as a "marijuana seeds exporter," and was quoted by *The Vancouver Sun:* "There isn't a single victim in my case, no one who can stand up and say, 'I was hurt by Marc Emery.' No one."

To many Canadians, the prospect of life imprisonment for the purveyor of marijuana seeds seems ludicrous. The leader of Canada's New Democratic Party has been photographed alongside Marc Emery and has vowed support for marijuana legalization. Canada's Green Party also favours this legislation.

Shouldn't life prison terms be reserved for those who directly threaten lives? They are not being considered for the CEOs of California "Ring of Fire" gun companies, which seed America's slums with low-cost handguns. Surely, many can trace their life-threatening injuries and the loss of relatives to the matériel traded by those death merchants. But America, at least Republican America, has always been passionate about The War on Drugs, including soft drugs.

How one feels about Marc Emery and the question of America's fairness in hunting him down has a lot to do with familiarity and history: What forms and grades of cannabis are on the streets and in the family rooms of the nation today? What place in society did the drug have historically?

Marijuana has long been valued in a variety of societies and countercultures. Recent studies, however, cast doubt on its reputation as a "soft drug." In the United Kingdom, scientists testing marijuana on healthy volunteers noted a marked difference in effect between the calming compound cannabidiol (CBD) and its better known constituent tetrahydrocannabinol (THC) that can produce temporary psychotic symptoms, including hallucinations and paranoid delusions, even in normal subjects. Clearly, cannabis is a complicated drug that excites interest on both sides of the law.

In late autumn 2006, the police raided a Toronto high-rise and seized six thousand plants – an operation that was just one of four hundred and fifty Ontario Provincial Police probes of illegal marijuana grow ops. Meanwhile, deep in an artificially lit, abandoned zinc mine, the Canadian government also grew cannabis plants. Its aim was to produce marijuana of standardized grade and strength for the treatment of a number of medical conditions. These include the disabling, painful muscular symptoms of multiple sclerosis and the agony of terminal cancer. Such split-brain attitudes towards marijuana are typical.

Cannabis preparations are largely derived from the female plant of cannabis sativa. The primary psychoactive constituent is 8-9 tetrahydrocannabinol. The THC content is highest in the flowering tops and declines in the leaves, lower leaves, stems and seeds of the plant. Marijuana (THC content 0.5%–5.0%) is prepared from the dried flowering tops and leaves; hashish (THC content 2%–20%) consists of dried cannabis resin and compressed flowers; and hashish oil may contain between 15% and 50% THC.

The THC content of marijuana on the street has risen over the decades, from an estimated 3.5% in the 1980s to as high as 8.5% in 2006. Thus, the marijuana used by boomer parents and by those who experimented with it when they were young, is a different drug from that used by their offspring.

In his fascinating, largely marijuana-sympathetic book *Cannabis: a History,* British author Martin Booth lists nicknames for marijuana: "grass, hash, weed, pot, dope, skunk, wacky baccy, cake, dank, muggles, gage, buddah, king bud, Mary Jane, cheeba, stuff, smoke, spinach, Mr. Alexander (or Mr. A.) and tea." Some names, such as "ganja" (Jamaican but derived from the Hindu) and "kif" (Arabic) have moved over into more general usage. My own adolescent contacts sometimes refer to the drug as "bud" or, quite fittingly from my point of view as a psychiatrist, "chronic."

There are also nicknames for marijuana cigarettes and pot paraphernalia. One can visit a "head shop," whether in London, Ontario, or London, England, and find a parallel universe of paraphernalia devoted to the recreational use of the products of the versatile cannabis plant. As of 2008, Toronto boasted stores with names like The Toronto Hemp Company (THC) and Queen Street's own Friendly Stranger Cannabis Culture Shop. Canadian teenagers could even order it online from services such as BudMail, since police cannot search your email without a warrant, and it would be delivered in unmarked, smell-proof, bubble-wrapped packages. Online purveyors tripped over one another boasting who has the purest, most potent product.

Recently, college kids have taken to using vaporizers, which cost anywhere between one hundred and fifty and six hundred dollars, to inhale the drug without having to endure the more irritating, high-temperature smoke. I was informed by one of my patients that this method works even better than using the less pricey bongs.

Cannabis is the most widely used illicit drug on the planet, accounting for half of all customs seizures. According to Booth, some one hundred and twenty countries report cannabis cultivation – 65% of all UN nations – compared with 20% that grow opium and 4% that grow coca bushes. However, in most counties, subgroups of daily cannabis users, be they Sufi Muslims or Jamaican Rastafarians, are viewed by the majority population as renegades or heretics, and are more tolerated than trusted.

As early as the eleventh century, powerful myths swirled around the use of cannabis, centring on the figure of Shiite Islamic dissident Hasan-e Sabbah, founder of a breakaway sect called the Nizari Ismailites. He was said to have dispatched political assassins across the Islamic world, allegedly young men pumped up on hashish and eager to perform martyrdom missions. Today, the veracity of so unlikely a use of hashish has been called into question, but the myth of the Assassins (*Hashshashin*) was established and spread throughout Europe by the returning Marco Polo. Such myths set the stage for more modern claims that cannabis products instilled a tendency to extreme violence in their users. Ironically, like Vietnam vets before them, Western soldiers returning from rotations in Iraq, Afghanistan and elsewhere in the Middle East are some of the heaviest users of cannabis, to relieve their pain or stress overseas.

Cannabis-derived hashish and marijuana are sometimes referred to as gateway drugs. Whether they open the doors of perception to meditative and religious experiences, or lead to experimentation with other, "harder" drugs has been hotly debated in many countries. The United States, for example, declared a now decades-old War on Drugs, a term coined by then-President Richard Nixon in 1971. This war has always been nebulous, partly because the use of cannabis got lumped in with that of opiates. Also, no distinction was made among the various grades of potency of cannabis-derived products. Whatever the specific targets of The War on Drugs, it resulted in more than one hundred thousand arrests in the United States the year after it was declared, and has since been a key factor in American foreign policy.

The anti-cannabis debate was freighted with social class concerns. The more affluent, White Protestant majority feared invasion by the foreign habits of migrant workers from countries where pot-smoking was endemic, such as the Orient, the Indian subcontinent, Mexico and islands in the Caribbean. The use of cannabis by the poor, unemployed and socially marginalized and by anti-authoritarian groups ranging from jazz and rock musicians to beats (beatniks) to campus activists, endowed marijuana enthusiasts with the cachet of social revolution. More recently, The War on Terror has focused attention on the relationship between drug money and the financing of terror groups. The blanket anti-drug thrust lumps cannabis products with more deadly street drugs such as heroin, cocaine, crystal meth, LSD and ecstasy (E). It should be said, that even if marijuana use does not usually lead to stronger drugs, many drug traffickers who deal in more potent and profitable street drugs got their start as small-time pushers of marijuana and hashish.

Harry J. Anslinger, the single appointed American official who ran the Federal Bureau of Narcotics (FBN) in the United States over several presidential terms, orchestrated a smear campaign that linked marijuana with social degradation and unspeakably violent criminal acts. This powerful anti-drug czar's views were taken up by media baron William Randolph Hearst and led to much purple journalism and anti-marijuana films like the B-movie classic *Reefer Madness*.

Those who propose decriminalizing cannabis products or advocate their outright legalization are quick to contrast them with two addictive, toxic, carcinogenic or violence-promoting substances long legal in our society: tobacco and alcohol. They argue that the mellowness and mirth promoted by marijuana are no threat to the population at large. They dispute the claims of health experts that suggest that marijuana, especially when used daily, reduces motivation and ambition, or that frequent use results in at least psychological, if not physiological addiction. They certainly dispute classifying marijuana alongside other heavy-duty Schedule I drugs, such as heroin and cocaine.

In my first encounters with the "fragrant cane," it took on mythic proportions. As a student in the ever-experimenting sixties, I watched in awe as trailblazing rebels slightly older than me lit up thick reefers, parked in huge university lots or back alleys, ever on the lookout for a police cruiser that could pull up at any moment. Several of these male friends went on to first-year university. There, mediocre grades obliged some to switch to a community college, while several dropped out of university, joined the work force or, if supported by wealthy parents, swelled the ranks of the affluent unemployed. One or two regular users were very bright lights who managed to maintain good grades against the odds and became esteemed and well-paid professionals in the community, though not leaders in their fields.

Although I partook in these pot-smoking circles, a cautious temperament and lack of personal funds never turned recreational, weekend use into a daily habit. To this day, I find it unpleasant to smoke anything and have joined Physicians for a Smoke-Free Canada. Even in the freewheeling sixties, I refrained from purchasing my own stash, and instead relied on smoking "OPs;" namely, joints belonging to Other People. Whether this was a portent of the future psychiatrist in me or the thriftiness of a child of Depression-era parents, I suspected that a "nickel or a dime bag or an ounce" of the stuff would beckon, luring me from my academic obligations and relationships into long, drawn-out contemplations of my navel.

After a while, I turned my back on the circle of marijuana smokers, having sensed that this was a drug difficult to use in moderation. Moreover, the vocabularies of many of my heavy-user friends seemed to be increasingly monosyllabic, a side effect that was anathema to a young man who wanted to become a writer.

The grades of available pot in the sixties and seventies were getting stronger, and I came to dislike the slightly paranoid feelings and the cartoon-character sense of self that complicated my pleasure in getting high with guilt about all the wasted money and time. I viewed driving a car while high as a dangerous exercise. The groovy elongation of time and space the drug provided I later found in mindfulness meditation. There would be no more "munchies," but how many middle-aged adults' weight or cholesterol levels make that a desirable side effect?

As a psychiatrist trained in working with children and adolescents, I grow increasingly uneasy about the downward drift in the age of kids first using street drugs. Studies have shown that about 40% of those who try any drug will develop a dependence on it. The lifetime risk of drug abuse or drug dependence is reduced between 4% and 5% for every year drug use is delayed. It is therefore very different when an eighteen-year-old tries a drug than when a thirteen-year-old does, and I've learned to ask the question of my teenaged patients, When was the first time you ever tried a cigarette, a drink, a joint ...

The marketing of some drugs to appeal to young teens and even tweens, by stamping potentially deadly E pills with little cartoon images or using the Joe Camel cartoon figure in cigarette ads, are beneath contempt. The ever-rising potency of street marijuana and its effect on still-developing adolescent brains is also of particular concern. An estimated 60% of first-time marijuana users are under eighteen-years-old, and the effects on still-developing brains of such a potent euphoriant have yet to be determined, since no one can conduct ethical prospective studies.

Having practised psychotherapy for thirty years, I have often seen the consequences of marijuana use in my patients and their families. I am wary about cannabis use, particularly by those under eighteen, and especially if the drug is used on more than a weekend, recreational basis or in combination with alcohol or other street drugs. In my clinical experience, the regular use of cannabis, especially in the more potent form of hashish, typically results in a significant decrease in academic test scores. In many cases, the difference may be between graduating from school and having to repeat years or even dropping out. The issue is of particular concern in an era when fewer boys than ever are making it to university. On a macroeconomic level, it also has implications for the productivity of the North American work force.

Teenagers who smoke marijuana in groups typically claim, "Everyone does it." In addition to the social need for approval from a select peer subgroup, many teens smoke marijuana as a rough-and-ready treatment for a sleep disorder, the most common type involving difficulty in initiating sleep, or "delayed onset sleep disorder." Some of these youngsters would be better off trying a health-food-store medication like melatonin or a prescription medication like clonidine in low doses. Many also have difficulty maintaining a good-enough baseline mood. They are often stimulus-seeking and easily bored. Others have obsessive traits that they find troubling. Some respond quite well to stimulant medication or to antidepressants, often in low to moderate doses, especially in combination with the insights derived from psychotherapy.

There are happily married couples who share a little dope on a regular basis. However, couples therapists often deal with troubled marriages where only one spouse partakes of drugs. In heterosexual couples, it is more often the male than the female. The recurring desertion the non-user feels when a partner trips out, individually or with smoke buddies, can lead to conflict, separation or divorce. The proportion of women who consult with doctors for depression and other health problems is far greater than that of men. It is likely that many of the missing men who are sad, fearful or in pain are self-medicating, whether with alcohol or other drugs. This subject is masterfully explored in a book by men's group therapist Terrence Real, titled *I Don't Want to Talk About It.*

The drug high is followed by a more protracted coming-off period of irritability, and thus, regular cannabis use can accentuate or at least complicate the treatment of pre-existing psychological disorders. As mentioned, there is growing concern about worsening the severity of conditions such as schizophrenia and attention deficit disorder (ADD). Indeed, one of the key conditions to rule out before diagnosing ADD is frequent marijuana use, which produces similar effects on concentration and the capacity for sustained work.

The effect of the marijuana high varies with the personality of the individual taking the drug. More extreme people are likely to react to cannabis intoxication or withdrawal in more extreme ways, particularly when the drug use is mixed with alcohol or other street drugs. Those who already suffer from psychiatric conditions, such as schizophrenia, bipolar disorder, depression or attention deficit disorder, frequently turn to psychoactive substances as a quick and reliable route to relaxation. Many people with chronic pain conditions also become regular users. An increasing number of people are contracting technology-related, painful neuromuscular problems, from carpal tunnel syndrome to repetitive strain injury to fibromyalgia. I suspect that many of these legions of stressed and distressed individuals, for whom conventional medical treatments offer only modest relief, drift into trying alternate herbal remedies, including the less than fully legal "fragrant cane," in their quest for symptom relief.

Regrettably, some self-proclaimed "psychiatric survivors" who describe being swamped by prescription medications later turn for relief to street drugs, but their daily use may perpetuate or worsen the very conditions they self-medicate.

As a poet and author, I am aware that many renowned creative writers, visual artists and musicians regularly used cannabis and other drugs. Many had co-existing psychiatric problems, and some used hashish or marijuana to periodically re-ignite their waning creativity. The famous jazz musicians of New Orleans, like the urban poor in general, used cannabis as an inexpensive way to achieve levity and release from the daily grind of living near or below the poverty line.

Canadian media scholar Marshall McLuhan remarked that LSD is "the lazy man's *Finnegans Wake.*" In this light, marijuana, hashish and cannabis may well be the lazy man's version of mindfulness meditation. I advise my young patients to totally avoid the more powerful, condensed forms of the substance, like hashish or hashish oil; to consider waiting until they are eighteen or older before trying marijuana; and if they are determined, to avoid more than occasional, recreational use. I have a similar view of alcohol, and believe that most forms of spirits, particularly of the tasteless variety, are the royal road to inebriation, liver and brain damage. In my view, "hard stuff" should be avoided by anyone with even a single first-degree alcoholic relative in their family tree.

Those who wish to introduce cannabis products into their lives may want to contemplate the following daunting list of its side effects from the 1998 seminar article "Adverse effects of cannabis" by Wayne Hall and Nadia Solowij in the British medical journal *The Lancet*. This exhaustive list may be more than ten years old, but it still applies today.

Acute effects:

- Anxiety and panic, especially in naive users.
- Impaired attention, memory and psychomotor performance while intoxicated.
- Possibly an increased risk of accident if a person drives a motor vehicle while intoxicated with cannabis, especially if cannabis is used with alcohol.
- Increased risk of psychotic symptoms among those who are vulnerable because of personal or family history of psychosis.

Chronic effects (uncertain but most probable):

- Chronic bronchitis and histo-pathological changes that may be precursors to the development of malignant disease.
- A cannabis dependence syndrome characterized by an inability to abstain from or to control cannabis use.
- Subtle impairments of attention and memory that persist while the user remains chronically intoxicated, and that may or may not be reversible after prolonged abstinence.

Possible adverse effects (to be confirmed):

- Increased risk of cancers of the oral cavity, pharynx and esophagus; leukemia among offspring exposed in utero.
- Impaired educational attainment in adolescents and underachievement in adults in occupations requiring high-level cognitive skills.

Groups at higher risk of experiencing these adverse effects:

- Adolescents with a history of poor school performance, who initiate cannabis use in the early teens, are at increased risk of using other illicit drugs and of becoming dependent on cannabis.
- Women who continue to smoke cannabis during pregnancy may increase their risk of having a low-birthweight baby.
- People with asthma, bronchitis, emphysema, schizophrenia and alcohol and other drug dependence, whose illnesses may be exacerbated by cannabis use.

As for stimulating creativity, many of the Romantic poets such as Keats and Shelley used opiates, and beat authors such as Allen Ginsberg and musicians from Louis Armstrong to John Lennon celebrated the use of pot. The right of social dissidents and their young followers to do so is championed by advocacy groups such as The National Organization for the Reform of Marijuana Laws (whose acronym is, paradoxically, NORML). Personally, I never wrote much of value while buzzed or stoned, though some writers claim a more positive experience.

Psychiatrists are not infrequently accused of pigeonholing people by societal expectations. In defence, I would say there are fewer habits that make for downward social mobility and achievement than the regular daily use of any euphoria-inducing drug, including marijuana. Professor George Patton, author of a ten-year study of the alcohol and marijuana use of Australian youth, used a touch of Aussie bluntness: "Cannabis really does look like the drug of choice for life's future losers." In my own psychiatric practice, I have frequently seen young people on a mix of marijuana and alcohol do self-destructive or inconsiderate things that seemed totally out of character.

Writing in *The Globe and Mail,* columnist Margaret Wente argued against outright legalization, claiming that it would be ill-advised to allow advertising agencies to step into the fray and sell ever more young people on trying marijuana. Advocates of legalization counter by saying there would be restrictions on ad firms similar to those now in place on cigarette and alcohol advertisers. They also want to see purveyors of the drug set up shop legally, so that users need not rely on connections affiliated with organized crime.

Clearly, mythic marijuana offers an inexpensive respite to many, as well as potential relief from some of the worst cases of human suffering. In its present incarnation, however, marijuana is more than just a soft drug, and its ever-increasing use should not be taken lightly, especially by the young or emotionally vulnerable. On the other hand, the Conservative government of Prime Minister Stephen Harper has tabled a legislation titled Bill C-26 which could mean prison terms for growers of a single marijuana plant, provided the purpose is for trafficking. Marijuana is nowhere near as dangerous to one's physical and mental health as a mandatory six-month-minimum stay in prison. The approach taken by a leader like Harper is the one argument I can think of in favour of outright legalization, as opposed to the decriminalization now effectively in place in Canada.

In the United States, such decriminalization exists in only a dozen more-enlightened states, and in all states, the people most likely to be charged with possession are from the most disadvantaged social groups. At the same time, abuse of *prescription* drugs, such as stimulants, flourishes, particularly among American university students, often by scamming Internet pharmacy outlets or actual drug stores. Young people may obtain prescription drugs from their doctors to sell or give to others, feigning symptoms likely to land them a prescription. The movie *Charlie Bartlett* is a send-up of such practices, set in an American public high school.

In December, 2008, *The Canadian Journal of Psychiatry* hosted a lively debate on policy reform in cannabis control. Doctors Kisely, Room and Hall argued for greater community investment in prevention, treatment and research of the cannabis problem. Kisely noted that, while the number of cannabis users looking for specialist help has doubled over the past decade, existing services still focus on opiates rather than on cannabis. He noted that greater reliance on law enforcement and other "supply-side" measures has failed to slow the increased use of cannabis, particularly among the young. By contrast, "demand-side" initiatives have been quite effective in anti-smoking strategies, such as increased taxation, restrictions on smoking in public areas and work spaces, bans on advertising and improved access to smoking cessation treatment, to the point where marijuana use often eclipses cigarette use in some surveys of Canadian youth.

"Demand-side" education on the harmfulness of street drugs is currently seen as less effective, but I would suggest that the main centres for role modelling addictive behaviours are family homes, where enlightened parental attitudes coupled with engagement and supervision can exert a marked effect on the age of onset and the extent of drug experimentation among the young. It is not unusual, in any peer group of teen pot smokers, to have one or two leaders who come from homes where the practice is either tolerated or covertly encouraged.

There will always be publicity-seeking, pro-cannabis adult role models like Vancouver's Prince of Pot, Marc Emery. Are his crimes truly victimless, or do users of his product suffer, as a group, from a million tiny cuts? Emery's case clearly also stirs issues of sovereignty, as many

Canadians believe that American attitudes on drugs should not dictate our own law enforcement. In the interview with Mr. Emery I saw on Canadian television, he came across as a well-spoken individual, with deep shadows around his eyes and the look of someone who had not slept well in years. A maverick entrepreneur and self-proclaimed freedom fighter, he is more concerned with altering people's relationships with what he considers a soft drug than grappling with the overall costs to society that might follow a substantial increase in use. Margaret Wente wrote that 17% of Canadians used pot over the past year. If true, her statement may help explain the country's lagging productivity.

That being said, Emery's seeds are in competition with arguably more lethal products which the United States turns a blind eye towards, such as cigarettes, alcohol – and firearms. If Marc Emery does have a point, it's that the concept of harm is painfully relative.

The United States is a country both very anti-drug and very pro-drug, similar to its split personality on the issue of interpersonal violence. The pharmaceutical industry, like the firearms industry, has been coddled, and there have been strong campaigns for expanding the use of pharmaceuticals, such as statins, antidepressants and even stimulant medications such as Ritalin and dextroamphetamine. Indeed the journal *Nature* recently offered a commentary article titled "Towards responsible use of cognitive-enhancing drugs by the healthy."

A conflicting notion can be set against Mr. Emery's plea for greater social diversity. Simple pot can interfere with the functioning of the inferior frontal cortex, the brain's paranoia centre, and centres of ambition tend to dwindle under its influence, while centres of passivity are switched on. Yet Marc Emery certainly does not lack in ambition. He has a vision of society "making love, not war," albeit a vision that centres on a particularly double-edged drug. His opposition to The War on Drugs parallels my own feelings about the equally fruitless War on Crime and aspects of the vaunted War on Terrorism, with its reprehensible use of torture, which inadvertently aggravate the very problems they seek to stamp out.

Can Marc Emery expect the greater society to sanction a product more potent than its 1960s incarnation? That is a subject for a careful cost/benefit analysis and a sober, morally informed, rather than moralizing, debate. At the centre of that debate, in my view, is the welfare of the nation's young people. We must ensure that legalization does not mean extending the lie of illicit drugs – that it is cool to regularly exit consensual reality and fall into a prolonged trance. The issue echoes the dilemma of parents whose children spend hours watching television or playing video games. Our youth are too inexperienced at life to regularly drift off into altered states where such fundamentals as time, space, food and complex social values no longer anchor the shared human project. Our future requires their full commitment, and any substance that offers altered states as their own reward must be judiciously limited.

Concerned citizens' groups, levels of government and the legal apparatus are not as equipped as parents to set such limits. However, to do so, parents must inform themselves of the many faces of marijuana. The wizened baby face of middle-aged Marc Emery is only one.

Meanwhile, because Canada has strict gun laws and the Americans have strict drug laws, there is a constant flow of Canadian pot southward and American guns northward. Some of the smugglers are interested equally in guns and pot. While to my mind, there is no comparison between the harm pot does and the harm guns do, the fact that marijuana lures guns into Canada makes it anything but a harmless drug. Marc Emery and other dealers play active roles in this big picture. They should assume their share of responsibility for helping to perpetuate it.

Masters of Their Universe

There is more to life than increasing its speed. – Mohandas Gandhi

The recent disappearance of fifteen-year-old Brandon Crisp of Barrie, Ontario, who graduated from Xbox to Xbox Live, and became addicted to the video game *Call of Duty*, raises issues about what may happen once cyberspace becomes a substitute for reality. As his father said: "It filled a void. He's a quiet boy. A lot of the kids who play these games are very quiet." Mr. Crisp then added, "This has become his identity, and I didn't realize how in-depth this was until I took his Xbox away ... that's like cutting his legs off." Brandon's mother confirmed the degree of obsession, saying she would hear her son conversing with other players over the Xbox Live network through a headset all hours of the night. Group audio software included with subscriptions to these games allows a game player to engage with a cybercommunity, even as he progressively withdraws from the community of family and friends.

Microsoft offered to match a twenty-five thousand dollar reward for information of Brandon's whereabouts, but they neither accepted any blame, nor were assigned any by Brandon's parents, despite the fact that Brandon's period of intensive gaming coincided with his skipping school and stealing money. Across the United States, many parents are less sanguine about the addictive aspects of video games and are suing the companies who make them.

Closer to the heartland of the gaming world, the government of South Korea took action after ten people in Internet cafés in South Korea suffered cardiopulmonary-related deaths – at least seven reportedly from online gaming. More than one thousand counsellors were trained and more than one hundred and ninety hospitals and clinics recruited for the treatment of Internet addiction, according to Dr. Jerald Block of the Oregon Health and Science University in Portland. Dr. Block has been lobbying to include Internet Addiction Disorder in the *Diagnostic and Statistical Manual of Mental Disorders* (also known as the *DSM*), a new version of which is due out in 2012. Dr. Block believes that nearly 90% of sufferers also have some other form of psychiatric disorder, and mental health experts put the prevalence of such problems among all computer users at likely between 5% and 10%, possibly as high as 20% among the younger set.

In the winter of 2008, Stanford University School of Medicine conducted a study on playing video games. It showed that the portion of the brain that generates feelings of reward, the mesocorticolimbic centre, was more stimulated in male than female players, which may be why, the authors speculated, men become addicted more easily. The research study authors designed a primitive video game where a vertical wall-like line divided the middle of the screen. Ten balls then appeared to the right of the screen and moved towards the wall. If a player clicked on the balls before they hit the wall, he or she would gain more territory. Though all the players figured this out, male players were more adept at determining which balls, the ones closest to the wall, had to be clicked to expand their territory and were able to gain more. With males being territorial animals, is it any wonder that so many video games involve battles and conquests?

Computers have the curious ability to encourage or amplify certain personality traits, and can synchronize with many aspects of brain functioning. This ability is the basis for several computer-assisted therapies offered to stroke patients, who suffer neurological and sensory deficits, to help as complex cortical "brain maps" get redrawn and long-lost functions are restored. In his book *The Brain That Changes Itself,* Dr. Norman Doidge describes a number of patients' personal triumphs when their rehabilitation was assisted by computer-facilitated interventions.

On the other side of the ledger, however, is the computer's ability to recreate in its user a hovering, relaxed state of mind – a powerful draw to any individual who finds his or her life stressful. "Cory," one of my highly intelligent patients addicted to the computer screen, explained it to me: "In general, I enjoy computer games without a lot of content, but that make you strategize. Those games make you think just a little but not too much, and I find myself returning to them whenever I'm stressed out, and that sucks up huge amounts of my time."

Another technology-hooked patient, a university student I'll call "Augie," whose parents are from Hong Kong, disappears into his favourite Japanese video game *Final Fantasy* (the number on the name of the game keeps changing, but I believe we are now at version twelve) He spends five, seven, ten hours at a stretch, and many of his fellow gamers are from the other side of the world, enticing him to stay up most of the night, then sleep through his morning classes the next day. Augie has had little experience socializing outside his family, though the avatars he steers through cyberspace master their world with grace and aplomb, moving him ever higher up the competence ladder. By contrast, some of the girls he used to woo in his college classes seemed either maddeningly coy to him or could see through to his insecurities, and put up daunting roadblocks on his quest for an intimate relationship.

Cory and Augie have very different levels of experience in the joys of sex, but both are immersed on a daily basis in the joy of *flow,* which Cory described nicely when he talked about that game with just the right amount of challenge. The mental state also called flow, characterized by full immersion, an energized focus and success in an activity, was first described by a psychologist with the mellifluous name Mihaly Csikszentmihalyi in the 1980s. His work revealed exactly what happens when athletes or other performers are in the groove, on the ball or in the zone. His books detail the quest by those who would train musicians, athletes, and even businessmen and video game designers to find the optimal balance between challenge and skills that facilitates a full immersion experience and avoids both anxiety, on the one hand (when challenges are greater than abilities) and boredom on the other (when abilities are greater than the challenges offered).

What makes flow highly effective within a narrow range of experience and ever so slightly mesmerizing? Here are some of the ingredients: clear goals, concentration and focus, a loss of self-consciousness (like many teenagers, Cory and Augie are, at times, exquisitely self-conscious), a distorted sense of time, direct and immediate feedback, a workable balance between ability level and challenge, an activity that is intrinsically rewarding (dopamine levels rise slightly with each success) and a focus of awareness that is narrowed down to the activity itself, which Csikszentmihalyi called action awareness merging.

Are flow seekers truly addicted, even if they are scoring little dopamine hits like those of pellet-rewarded rats striking a feeding bar? How many have underlying psychological problems? Few in clinical practice will dispute that as the Internet expands into more and more areas of daily life (MSN, Facebook, MySpace, IM, YouTube, chat rooms, eBay, Pro Line, blogs, email, Twitter, etc.), the claims on one's pool of hours is astronomical.

The criteria for an Internet addiction disorder, quoted from that mildly addictive website, Wikipedia, might include aspects of the following. They originally appeared in a joke posted by Dr. Ivan Goldberg in 1995, as a parody of the strict format used by psychiatry's *Diagnostic and Statistical Manual of Mental Disorders:*

1. Tolerance, involving a need to spend increased amounts of time on the computer in order to achieve satisfaction, and a markedly diminished effect with continued use of the same amount of time on the Internet.
2. Withdrawal phenomena, in which a cessation in Internet use leads to agitation, anxiety, obsessive thinking about what is happening on the Internet, fantasies or dreams about the Internet and voluntary or involuntary typing movements of the fingers. The symptoms cause distress to the surfer and impairment in social, occupational or other areas of function.
3. The Internet is accessed more often for longer periods of time than was intended, causing the addict to neglect responsibilities at work and the needs of family at home.
4. There is a persistent desire or unsuccessful efforts to cut down or control Internet use.
5. An inordinate amount of time is spent in activities related to Internet use.
6. Frequent talks about the Internet in daily life.
7. Important family, social, occupational or recreational activities are given up or reduced because of Internet use.
8. Internet use is continued despite knowledge of having a persistent or recurrent physical, family, social, occupational or psychological problem likely to have been caused by or exacerbated by Internet use, such as sleep deprivation, marital difficulties, lateness for early morning appointments, neglect of duties or feelings of abandonment experienced by significant others.

In North America, scores of boys and teenaged males, whether truly addicted or not, spend hours playing video games, such as one of the many versions of *World of Warcraft, Halo, Final Fantasy, EverQuest* and *Grand Theft Auto.* The phenomenon warranted an episode on the TV series *South Park,* in which a number of *World of Warcraft* devotees become distressed when an invader of their video game keeps randomly killing off characters. (He turns out to be an oversized adult male living in his mother's basement.) The kids resolve to beat this guy by logging a total of seven hundred hours at the game. They chant things like "We must save the world … of *Warcraft!*" By the end of their mission, all the game playing has left them fat and unable to move.

In a way, TV addiction is easier to document and quantify than Internet addiction, partly because the Internet pervades the workplace and so many mundane tasks – email long ago displaced the typewritten letter, for better or worse. Neuropsychologist Gary Small, author of *iBrain: Surviving the Technological Alteration of the Modern Mind,* believes that as many as 20% of the younger generation have what he calls "pathological" patterns of Internet use.

Youth whose time becomes dominated by the computer screen are not infrequently, but by no means exclusively, lonely individuals with marginal social skills. However, in *iBrain,* Gary Small speculates that even normal young people setting down ever-increasing neural pathways to respond to technology are affected. Simultaneously, they begin to lose interpersonal-skills pathways necessary for developing social skills, such as picking up cues from the faces or body language of peers and even family members. He posits that some kids are much more sensitive than others to this techno overstimulation, suggesting an interplay between individual genetics and the new high-tech environment. They may have problems focusing attention that result from not using portions of the brain needed to grasp the big picture. Instead, they substitute a constantly scanning and free-flowing attention that rarely settles on any one thing for more than a second.

The teenage years are a key time for the development of skills such as empathy. The frontal lobes that are a vital part of planning and thinking ahead are also in the process of maturing through the process of myelination. There is also a neuronal "pruning" that takes place throughout childhood and adolescence, in which weak or damaged neurons are removed in order to improve the networking efficiency of certain parts of the developing brain.

Teenagers who have little success with peers may compensate by getting the highest scores in their game and by interacting with a number of other gamers from around the world, few, if any of whom they will ever actually meet. They send their avatars into cyberspace and substitute role play for the rejection-fraught, step-by-step social roles of the real world. Girls who get hooked are more likely to while away their time on MSN, IM and Facebook than to role play on *EverQuest.*

As a therapist, I became convinced long ago that the Internet has unique potential for eroding human fitness and productivity, with its incredible ability to be used as a "trancing" device. Given the Aha! response received by the Pixar film *WALL·E,* in which computer-screen-addicted, oversized adults wile away their time in mindless bliss, my concerns about the booted life seem to be shared by many others.

Nothing else on earth responds to a human command with the speed of a computer processor. Cyber relationships offer subjectively daring forays at relatively low risk (though to read about the growing "cyberbullying" you might not think so). Neil Postman's warning about excessive TV and media engagement, *Amusing Ourselves to Death,* has never felt more prescient.

Yet Sino-Japanese Nintendo or Play Station or Wii are not consciously designed to undermine the health of North American – or of Chinese and Japanese – youth, even if they have that effect on the vulnerable. Nor is it a new thing to cast a wary eye on new entertainment technologies and their perfidious effects on youth. Social commentators in the 1950s felt that comic books were too violent and feared they would irreparably corrupt the youth of their day.

A stand-on-one-leg history of video gaming would begin with *Tennis for Two,* created in 1958 by William Higinbotham. In 1962, Steve Russell at MIT invented *Spacewar!,* the first game for a computer. In 1967, followed the first game for a television set. A quantum leap occurred with the creation of the video arcade game *Pong,* by two men who went on to found Atari computers. In 1972, the first commercial video game console that could be played at home appeared, called *The Odyssey,* programmed with twelve games. In 1980, Atari's *Asteroids* and *Lunar Lander* were the first two games to be registered in the copyright office. This early period is sometimes referred to as "The Dark Ages" of video gaming.

The 1980s saw the advent of Nintendo and its Game Boy, invented by Gunpei Yokoi. By 1994, more than 70% of video games released in North America were designed in Japan, and local social mores around issues such as gender inequality heavily influenced gaming goals and game content. The *Super Mario* series heavily penetrated the educational market. One of the first RPGs (role-playing games, not rocket-propelled grenades) was *Final Fantasy,* followed by many subsequent imitations and versions, such as the infamously addictive *EverQuest.* Whether in a strategy or role-playing game, the feature of real-time interaction (RTI) with other gamers gives the isolated player added reason to persist in trying to outperform opponents who are, as the song goes, "somewhere out there."

Many early computer games offered little freedom, assigning the player a single character and highly scripted scenarios. The initial major first-person shooter (FPS) game was *Doom,* which focused on killing demons in a Mars-like scenario that resembled hell, while subsequent FPS games such as *Halo* featured warring with aliens. Later games such as *Grand Theft Auto* allow for an "open sandbox," free-for-all style of play.

Many studies exploring the link between violent behaviour and video games have been inconclusive, while Jack Thompson and other critics of the industry have frequently advocated for such a link on FOX News. Defenders argue that video games provide another outlet for the same aggression indulged by watching violent movies or television.

They argue it is better for kids to take out their anger on pixilated people than real human beings.

While no studies have definitively linked FPS games to actual violent crimes, the teenaged shooters at Columbine showed clear media influences. In a bizarre twist, their horrific attack on their school served as the template for a video game based on the massacre, opening the door to possible "me-too" crimes. Some studies have demonstrated a link between computer games and non-specific aggressive and bullying behaviour.

Clearly the industry has seen an explosion of titles and small independent companies. However, from the start, it has been preoccupied with outer space, various forms of martial combat and weapons. Some of the many games centring on the US army are so realistic they are used for recruitment and training.

Would socially awkward, phobic, depressed, attention-deficited or autistic kids be better off unplugged from their cyber iron lungs? After all, kids with learning disabilities, tired of their academic limitations, can compensate grandly by becoming wizards of cyberspace. Many bored, gifted kids find the computer a garden of never-ending delights, and some will read anything and everything, so long as it is not on a curriculum.

In a multi-channel, cable-TV universe with BlackBerry addicts obsessing about the latest news on frenetic news channels like FOX or CNN, and younger users text-messaging on their cell phones or tracking the latest developments on 'reality TV,' perhaps we should talk about something more: Electronic Media Disorder, from which most of us suffer, though some to a more clinically significant degree.

A recent Kaiser Foundation study found that young people eight to eighteen exposed their brains daily, on average, to a staggering eight point five hours of digital and video sensory stimulation from television, video games and the computer. Indeed, the American Academy of Pediatrics advises against television and video watching for children under the age of two.

It would be wise to think twice before giving your son or daughter a TV and a computer for the bedroom, particularly if they are insidiously logging on for more hours as time goes by. It always pays to take an interest in the content of the games your kids are engaged in. Often the earlier levels of a game contain far less violence and sex than the more advanced levels. First-person shooter (FPS) video games are a terrible idea if your son is a loner who is being bullied or, if for some reason, you keep a loaded firearm in your home.

Remember that shopping for hard-core porn these days is as easy as shopping for popcorn. You don't need futurist Faith Popcorn to predict that easy access is not good news for kids, or young and even middle-aged adults with poor social skills or those suffering from anxiety, depression or addiction.

There are many other ways of shrinking one's universe to a more manageable size. Ethnic and religious communities try to do so for their younger members, as do community centres with recreational programs, and such arts institutions as museums, dance and art schools and conservatories of music. Endlessly engaging our youth in a fantasy universe filled with high-octane violence smacks of supplying them with soma from the book *Brave New World,* at a cost to their physical health and real-life, real-time relationships.

Not everyone would agree. *NOW Magazine* reporter Mike Smith asked an outreach coordinator of a violence intervention project (VIP) in Toronto what kids from disadvantaged neighbourhoods really need, between jobs, to keep them productively occupied. What would work better than their hanging out on the corner and resenting the cops, whom they see as doing little more than harassing dark-skinned youth dressed a certain way. "If not police, then what's needed in their neighbourhoods?" asked Smith. The worker replied, "Video games. Just somewhere to go and get to do what other kids do at home."

When Chinese piano progidy Lang Lang visited Toronto, one of his first enquiries was the whereabouts of a good video-game arcade. A study has found that laparoscopic surgeons who played video games made fewer errors. There are also individuals with neuroanatomical or neurophysiologic differences, such as those who have autism, who gravitate towards using computers and who find staying for too long in the consensual space that most people view as reality to be over- or understimulating, or simply oppressive. For such people, a caveat about the sheer number of hours spent on a computer, and what is being lost in the process, may sound like nothing more than undue pressure to conform.

Having said that, those of us who have close interpersonal relationships may forget how excruciatingly lonely the urban world can be for those young people who fall out of touch with their families, yet who fail to intimately connect with their peers. For them, banding together with others they experience only in a shared-audio world, to master a quest in a dragon- or alien-strewn environment may feel much more compelling than wandering a shopping mall, trying in vain to connect with another human being. It is ironic that the more hours such young people spend 'relating' to others in cyberspace, the worse their ability to connect becomes, as they seem increasingly weirder to their less addicted peers, whom they are often desperate to impress.

In the words of *iBrain*'s Gary Small: "My position on video games is my position on technology. 'Let's understand it and use it with balance.'" Towards this end he suggests establishing more time for family togetherness and putting the home computer in a shared space.

He then adds that the next techno wave will be a brain-computer interface, where people with electrodes on their foreheads control the computer with their thoughts. In addition to stimulating thoughts in me about movies like *The Matrix,* I can almost hear my mother's voice pointedly asking, "What do you need it for?" But then, she would have thought the same of the computers, cell phones and other gadgetry we use in our daily attempts to master the new information age which we find ourselves plugged into.

Note: Cory and Augie are a composite of three real-life patients, whose identities have been appropriately disguised.

How Pernicious is Pornography?

Strung out between romance and pornography it is no longer clear what men and women want to use each other for. – Adam Phillips

In the fall of 2008, actor David Duchovny signed himself into a sex addiction rehabilitation clinic for several weeks, shortly after he starred in a TV series called *Californication.* He expressed remorse towards his lovely, fellow-actor wife Téa Leoni, soon to become his ex-wife, and their two children.

You won't find sex addiction, not yet anyway, in the psychiatric field's *Diagnostic and Statistical Manual of Mental Disorders* or *DSM.* However, any expert who treats such a condition will attempt to soothe the lust addict's overactive limbic system and will likely recommend starting the healing with a long period of abstinence.

In his book, *The Brain That Changes Itself,* Dr. Norman Doidge reviews the many ways the brain can gain new functions to make up for those lost in strokes and other brain disorders. In a chapter called "Acquiring Tastes and Loves," he reminds us that the development of different "sexual tastes" contributes to the tremendous sexual variation among us.

Beyond those who are heterosexual, homosexual or bisexual there are also straight and gay people who identify themselves as sadists or masochists, or part of the bondage/discipline, dominance/submission, sadism/masochism (BDSM) community. They try to keep their diverging sexual interests "safe, sane and consensual," and hope to set up their meetings in a manner that avoids accidentally encountering actual criminal predators who intend to inflict serious physical injury.

Variation in sexual practice that involves an acquired taste for pain as part of pleasure remains controversial, and a 2002 article by Daphne Merkin on the joys of being spanked soon became a *source de scandal.* Even more unmentionable are variations in sexual taste that centre on a predilection for nude children, especially since society views the duty to protect children from sexual exploitation, let alone predation, as paramount.

Most people do not think of such exotica when they contemplate the increasingly mainstream world of pornography. The average person who accesses pornography tries not to trouble himself or herself with its wider social implications, viewing the activity as nothing more than an escape into good, unclean fun. It gets more complicated, however, when pornography rears its head in the family situation.

The advertising of sexualized toys and clothing to prepubescent girls, taken up in the book *So Sexy So Soon* by Diane E. Levin and Jean Kilbourne, made one mother lament, "Try buying a gift for a toddler girl sometime. The clothes look like mini-hooker garb, and the toys are nothing but Bratz, Barbie and other style/beauty-oriented toys." The Miley Cyrus picture scandal highlighted the extent to which nine-year-old girls emulate the teen and even adult sexual images bombarding them on television and at their local retail outlet, in a culture increasingly influenced by porn. While most people consciously deplore the making and use of kiddie porn, few people have spoken out against the tarting up of little girls by the fashion industry.

If men and women are not entirely sure where they stand on the issue of pornography, it's partly because no one wants to seem like a prude or a killjoy overly keen on censorship. To many avid male users, the deluge of porn on the Internet is no cause for alarm. It offers delicious eye candy, which they can sneak at home and occasionally at work, or perhaps at a quick stop at the strip club or during moments of "What-happens-in-Vegas" bliss.

But another take on pornography views its makers as more sinister, as brain re-shapers as much as smut peddlers. We were warned about the porn industry's anti-women slant in the 1981 Canadian indie film *Not a Love Story.* It's easy to imagine that being a pornstar and submitting to long bouts of sex on cue, involving the insertion of long-nailed fingers into both sexual orifices can't be all pleasure. Nor is it likely that most pornstars are inherently masochistic, and into what the BDSM community might call "consensual objectification."

In the more recent movie *Zack and Miri Make a Porno,* reviewed by David Denby in *The New Yorker,* a porn movie is a potential source of much-needed cash for two financially strapped young friends. The movie plays up porn as largely a spoof of both high and low culture. This benign view of pornography is in stark contrast with the feminist view of porn as the predacious exploitation of women, the theme of *Not a Love Story.*

In the real world, some people arrive at an anti-porn stance only after overexposure to it. They may lose patience with the repetitive, inaccurate and degrading images of women, images which can have consequences for viewers, their partners and the quality of their relationships. Misgivings may not set in until the habitual viewer senses the habit escalating out of control, the material becoming increasingly extreme, or a real-life sexual partner, when there is one, feeling neglected.

The user, more often a male, may also realize that the same lurid fare he is hooked on is also easily available to his teenage son and prepubescent daughter, who may stumble upon it accidentally during porn pop-ups that blight their web-surfing. A young child or teen may catch a parent masturbating before a computer screen, or find evidence of the activity that the parent forgot to hide. A father may erase his computer's surfing history, empty his internet cache and even reset his browser, giving the home computer the equivalent of permanent amnesia and may accidentally wipe out internet files that were part of his child's homework.

A worse interface between pornography and real life occurs when a psychologically vulnerable man has to ward off thoughts about his babysitter, niece or even his daughter or her teenaged friends, thoughts that intrude on his mind like the garish pop-ups that threaten to spill across the screen of the office computer. Thoughts that arrive unbidden and that are not easily dismissed can take on a discomforting obsessive quality, even when their content is supposed to be pleasurable, and especially when they are extreme even by porn standards.

In her book *Pornified,* subtitled *How Pornography Is Damaging Our Lives, Our Relationships and Our Families,* Pamela Paul, *Time* magazine journalist and no friend of pornography, canvasses American opinion on the subject. She commissioned the first nationally representative poll on the subject. The *Pornified*/Harris Interactive poll asked such questions as, "Does pornography improve the sex lives of those who look at it? Is pornography cheating? Do you believe all men look at pornography? How does pornography affect the children who view it?"

Ms. Paul differentiates between sexuality and its artistic representation, often termed erotica, and pornography, what she terms "the commercialized means to arousal." She is convincing when she states that the porn industry has, at least in more liberal circles, won its battle to deliver increasingly lurid fare worldwide, with unfettered access to most homes that have the Internet. In mid-October 2008, I entered the word "sex" on Google's search engine and came up with seven hundred and twenty million hits. Another search, linking sex with synonyms for violence, yielded more than a third as many.

Ms. Paul points out the effect of porn having gone mainstream: it comes to shape and create what people desire, rather than merely reflect it. Thus, many who use porn typically start out with, say, images of naked women or men, only to drift to images of actual intercourse, then multiple partners and, all too often, images of young children, men and women eliminating on one another (favourites of both the Marquis de Sade and Adolf Hitler) and women coupling with animals. Japanese *bukkake* porn may involve several men ejaculating on one woman or a woman being forced to ingest a jar of semen, in what most Westerners would view as a perversion of the "money shot" that often ends the banal sequences of everyday pornography. These indelicacies are often "just a click away" from the more standard-fare images viewers started out intent on enjoying. For many men, simple curiosity can escalate to delving into forms of sexual activity they had no idea they were interested in.

To what extent, then, does porn tickle us by tapping into how we are secretly wired? Didn't Freud point out that, in the Unconscious, anything and everything goes? Or is the medium now powerful enough to actually rewire our sexual circuitry? As with the effects of video games, the answer may depend in part on the sheer amounts of time spent at the activity. Most people enjoy being horny. But there is a time and place, and the mission of the financially driven pornographer is to expand the boundaries of time and place of the sexual realm.

Ms. Paul anchors her book in vignettes and personal interviews showing that porn can paradoxically desensitize even young men to sexual imagery, to the point where anything less than extremes leaves them understimulated. They may become prematurely jaded with real-life, real-time sex and either neglect their partners' sexual needs or may have to prop up their flagging interest with Viagra. The essence of porn is masturbation to a particular set of images, soon to be discarded in favour of fresh images in the next masturbation session, which may take place the same day. Even juicy fantasy favourites become ho-hum with unlimited exposure.

Ms. Paul insists that the plasticized women in porn movies make men increasingly breast-centric and disparaging of their real-life partners' physical attributes and limitations, to the delight and profit of the burgeoning plastic-surgery, breast-enhancement industry.

Women in porn films are portrayed as always willing to do men's bidding, to take swift and absolute delight in having their faces and bodies plastered with semen (again, the so-called "money shots" *dénouements* in most porn movies). They seem unfazed by violent words and extreme or risky physical acts perpetrated on them, from double-penetration to unprotected anal sex to fisting, to the use of a variety of potentially hazardous, inserted instruments of the "Don't try this at home" variety. Over time, frequent porn viewers, especially young viewers with little or no real-life experience, may come to mistake these frenetic shenanigans for normal sex, and strive to emulate it, with predictable results.

Ms. Paul does not flinch from quoting the actual words of hardcore porn users and from actual porn scripts. She explains that, without such faithful description, her readers, like many wives and girlfriends, may underestimate the extremes porn goes to in order to remain at the very edge of what is acceptable in our "pornified" society.

In the words of one of the many experts in Ms. Paul's book, "The massive exposure of men to the portrayal of women as sex-crazy creatures who move from partner to partner is thought to make women seem unworthy of attention and care in an enduring relationship." Even though the women of porn are often shaved, groomed and prepped to look like young, "barely legal" girls, this is hardly the image of women most men would want their wives or sisters, let alone their daughters, to emulate. Most people want to be horny some of the time, but what is it like to be too horny or horny at very inappropriate times? That, alas, is not the pornographer's concern. To paraphrase the Tom Lehrer song about rockets:

> Once the (penis goes) up,
> who cares where (it comes) down
> That's not my department,
> Says Wernher Von Braun.

Like most tolerant liberals, Ms. Paul adopts a "censure-not-censor" solution. She is aware that those on both the far right and the far left who oppose the rampant spread of pornography may have hidden agendas, if they come by their strong reactions to it honestly. Some on the right, for example, are homophobic and eager to legislate, not only against homosexual acts, but against the distribution of sex education materials. That households who only discuss sex in terms of abstinence may have an elevated rate of teen pregnancy is a contradiction many seem willing to live with, as in the family example made famous by the Sarah Palin candidacy.

As a psychiatrist who works with children and adolescents, I found Ms. Paul's chapter "Born into porn: kids in a pornified culture" particularly compelling, and would endorse many of Levin and Kilbourne's solutions in *So Sexy So Soon*. I suspect that the increasing number of formerly upstanding men brought down in porn and even kiddy porn scandals may represent a psychological entrapment to which both highly repressed, conservative men and highly liberal, more experimental middle-aged males are equally prone. The instantaneous, inexpensive and often gratis rushes of commitment-free sexual excitement on the Net can come to have the dopamine-releasing qualities of crack cocaine. As in other addictions, the *travailles* of everyday family living are increasingly neglected, and real-life, real-time, formerly loving relationships may deteriorate.

One porn website, which starts out with the carefully worded disclaimer that its images are meant to be used "as sexual aids, to provide sexual education and to provide sexual entertainment" offers its viewers, just a click of the mouse later, a screen that blares, "Home of the A—hole Milkshake, The most extreme sh-t you'll ever see. See why the US government is after us!"

Is this merely an honest effort to cash in on our inherent "neuroplasticity," or might such "extreme sh-t" fare, if it really wins us over, forge in us a new paraphilia? Can porn transform us into fetishists simply by bombarding a fetish-prone area of our brains, especially if Freud's "fixation points," based on powerful childhood experiences, already inclined us in that direction? Even if we are latent fetishists, to what extent do we want our fascinating paraphilias to become the lynchpins of our identity? Just how much psychic energy dare we devote to them? Perhaps even the immoderate is meant to be sampled in moderation.

Many people share fantasies and attitudes that overlap with those of sex offenders. A review article by J. Paul Federoff in *The Canadian Journal of Psychiatry* pointed out that "among college students in one study, 51% indicated they would rape a woman if they could get away with it and, perhaps most controversially, 25% of the male and female college students in the sample thought women would enjoy being raped if no one knew about it." Clearly, porn's sensibility is either prescient or pervasively influential. Federoff adds, "Most rapes involve the use of alcohol. In one representative study, according to 61% of the victims, the offender was under the influence of alcohol. It is unknown whether the percentages of students apparently approving of rape in the previous study would have been higher had the surveys been done after the respondents had consumed alcohol."

"Neurons that *fire* together *wire* together," Dr. Doidge repeatedly reminds us in his book. He also warns continually that whole cognitive functions can be lost with disuse, as in "Use it or lose it." Perhaps pornography is powerful enough to rewire our proclivities and make the less frenzied pace of real-life, real-time sex fall by the way. If you believe that, you might move closer to the view that pornography is indeed pernicious, and decide to trade in your personal freedom to look at whatever they are serving on the high-definition TV screen for the more three-dimensional challenges and rewards of a flesh-and-blood person in an actual bed.

In the end, it comes down to the question, "What do we want to fill our minds with?" How much of that pie graph of mental contents should be devoted to images of sexual pie? How easy is it to switch off such images? What higher-level thoughts or images are they displacing?

I once asked a patient of mine whose parents are Orthodox Jewish, if he watches much pornography. He answered, "Very little. I find it embarrassing. You have to be able to forget that they're real people, and I just can't manage to do that." I wondered for a moment if this represented a failure or a triumph of his imagination.

These are moral issues, but they also concern the practical issue of how to lead a good-enough life, while keeping in check the ability of others to keep jerking at the strings of our animal nature.

Adventures in Alternative Medicine

A lot of quacks are out there, both inside and outside organized medicine. Of course, many empathic, devoted practitioners also hang out their shingles and treat people as full human beings who happen to be in distress. Allow me to share my fifteen-year experience winding a less than fully functioning body through the health care maze.

I have a poorly understood disorder for which conventional medicine has until recently provided few effective treatments. In such circumstances, the usefulness of what a patient or client or health care consumer receives, and often pays for out of pocket, depends on the luck of the draw; that is, the therapist's knowledge base and inclinations, and the patient's ability to master and to tolerate the treatment.

Mine was one of two increasingly common disorders that "fall between the cracks of what doctors can offer": fibromyalgia and myofascial pain. The first condition can affect as much as 2% of the population, with a nine to one ratio of women to men, while my disorder, let's label it posture problems resulting in myofascial pain syndrome, seems to affect both sexes equally.

Fifteen years ago, while in my early forties, after a year of zealous overuse of a cross-country ski machine, I developed pain and numbness in my lower back and hips, and tingling that went into my feet. Thinking I must have a protruding spinal disk, I navigated the usual medical channels. My family doctor examined me, referred me to a neurologist to rule out multiple sclerosis, since I hail from Winnipeg, a high MS area, then to an orthopaedic surgeon, and side-trips for a computerized axial tomography (CAT) scan, electromyograph (EMG), much-coveted magnetic resonance imaging (MRI) of the thoracic and lumbar spine and even a CT-myelogram that involved getting a spinal tap.

During this initial medical work-up I missed only three days from my office, but my schedule was dotted with health care appointments. Early morning and leisure hours also became crowded with specialized exercises, meditation on a prayer rug or yoga mat and, if I could manage, therapeutic walks. Always an active person who had enjoyed walking, swimming and jogging, I had never viewed myself as the physical culturalist I was becoming. Particularly vexing was my growing inability to drive for long or to carry any weight without symptoms in my feet. It was also difficult to explain at parties where I dragged my Obus Forme padded seat.

One reason why women live longer than men is that men avoid going to the doctor. This may not be just because of the intrusions of the physical examination, but due to the fact that men are reluctant to be examined at all, whether by physicians or government accountants. Yet medicine, alternative or conventional, is fraught with moments where one is physically manipulated or left to the tender mercies of a practitioner hoped to be competent.

After assorted inconclusive medical findings, I wound up at a unique Clinic of Injury and Disease Response (CIDR), run by a psychiatrist with a dual background in family medicine and psychiatry and his family-practitioner wife. Using high-tech computer software, they thoroughly tested my muscle strength under varying conditions, analyzed the results and pronounced my problem to be myofascial pain syndrome, with some traits of fibromyalgia.

Looking back, I realized that these problems had dogged me since my early medical school days. Back then, I awoke to a swelling in my neck that eventually convinced a specialist and his team to operate. Since it was just a fibrocystic nodule, the fluctuating soft-tissue mass disappeared as soon as the scalpel cut. It would also have yielded to a much less invasive treatment, such as "dry needling," and maybe even to benign neglect, but how was I to know?

Once the surgeons were finished with me, neither they nor my family doctor had anything more to offer. Whatever the problem was, it went into remission, and I returned to my studies. In those days, many doctors did not believe in soft-tissue disorders. Many still don't, despite their inclusion as bona fide illnesses in the official International Classification of Diseases, the ICD-10.

Fibromyalgia typically involves a heightened sensitivity to pain, as well as abnormally light "non-restorative sleep" that aggravates and weakens the muscles. Myofascial pain, if improperly treated, can produce equal amounts of disability. The disorder is caused by factors, which may include the following, as cited in a brochure of The National Fibromyalgia Partnership, called *Myofascial Pain due to Trigger Points:*

- Unaccustomed eccentric exercise or repetitive exercise syndromes.
- Hypermobility syndromes (to the layman, "double-jointedness").

- Forward head posture (jutting-jaw syndrome).
- Static overload (stressful positions held for prolonged periods of time, in my case sitting for long periods as both a therapist and an author).
- Sacroiliac joint dysfunction.
- Muscle imbalance (mechanical asymmetries).
- Pelvic torsion-related pain, etc.

A wide variety of non-mechanical medical conditions, such as hormonal and metabolic disorders, may make it worse.

Saddled with a non-life-threatening but often painful condition, I looked for relief outside conventional medicine, which had little to offer. Some days my many "trigger-points" made me think of St. Sebastian, discussed elsewhere in this book, who was pierced by multiple arrows. Tiny doses of old-fashioned antidepressants called tricyclics could turn down the pain tap, but they produced a sense of unreality that only compounded the sensory cloudiness known to sufferers as "fibro-fog."

Alternative medicine offered a wide array of practitioners who bullishly promised me full symptom relief.

Here's how the alternative encyclopedia, Wikipedia, defined alternative medicine at the time of this writing:

> **Alternative medicine** includes practices that differ from conventional medicine. A typical definition is "every available approach to healing that does not fall within the realm of conventional medicine." Commonly cited examples are homeopathy, naturopathy, chiropractic and herbal medicine.
>
> Alternative medicine practices may be based on unconventional belief systems or philosophies, biological data and observations or biochemical principles, and some may not follow the scientific method. They may incorporate spiritual, metaphysical or religious underpinnings, untested practices, pre-modern medical traditions or newly developed approaches to healing. If an alternative medical approach, previously unproven according to orthodox scientific or regulatory methodologies, is subsequently shown to be safe and effective, it may then be adopted by conventional practitioners and no longer considered "alternative."

Generally speaking, alternative or "complementary" medicine venues are well-lighted, airy and cheerful places, compared with many fluorescent-lit clinics and hospitals. But then, few in the waiting room are there for such urgent treatments as setting a fractured bone or undergoing dialysis.

If smiles are not breaking out in the waiting room, it is because patients know they are paying for the treatments. Suffering from protean, fluctuating conditions like fibromyalgia, they have already tried a number of therapists and know the score. A new practitioner may help reduce the level of their pain and suffering, but cannot offer a cure. Of course, much conventional medicine is the same. Not even those who receive a kidney transplant leave the specialist's office with brand new kidneys.

In my health care Odyssey to date I have yet to consult with a homeopath or naturopath. Nor, all the rage these days, have I hired a personal trainer. However, I have received several bouts of physiotherapy, numerous shiatsu and more standard Swedish massages and two rounds of chiropractic. I have been outfitted with orthotics by a podiatrist who 'adjusted' them every few weeks, and in recent months have even purchased a sub-infrared sauna. Other unequivocally helpful devices have included the Obus Forme seat, for use on hard wooden chairs and uneven, sinking sofas (I have no use for their famous back rest) and a device called a Thera Cane for self-administering pressure to muscle trigger points.

Let me start with the most hands-on, invasive treatment. Not long after my condition flared up during my forties, I visited a female chiropractor on a fashionable section of Toronto's Bloor Street, whom a patient of mine recounted had helped her learn to walk again. Relatively young, but not inexperienced, she pushed down so briskly and firmly on my lower back that I needed several months to fully recover.

Years later, regardless, I visited another chiropractor, a charismatic, chatty and eager cowboy healer, to help with my shoulder problems, 'tennis elbow' and 'golf elbow' (although I play neither sport). Also, too much typing under poor ergonomic conditions had caused some repetitive strain injury (RSI) in my forearms. As he snapped my limbs or upper back into place, he declared, "That's exactly what I wanted!" The jerky nature of these 'adjustments' alarmed me, and I considered instead returning to the kinder, gentler waters of physiotherapy and massage.

However, after slipping down three ice-glazed stairs outside my home, I came back with what felt like a double whiplash of both trapezius muscles. Once more, he did his springy snaps, and I felt remarkably better. However, similar twisting motions of my elbow, while tonic for my RSI forearms, seemed to give me a "trick elbow." That's the hitch with many complementary, alternative treatments: one leaves the practitioner's office improved in some ways but hurting more in others. I got out of the chiropractic net while I still could.

Since then, I've heard several chiropractor stories. While sensational tales of fatal strokes following chiropractic neck manipulation are very rare, those of unintended setbacks "caused" by this group of practitioners seem to me rather common. Having said that, I know many people "swear by" rather than swear at their chiropractors. Some chiropractors are also well versed in homeopathy or naturopathic medicine. Very conservative about performing adjustments, they take a lot of time to prepare more physically vulnerable patients for any kind of manoeuvres.

Perhaps any discipline that makes you sign your consent before treatment could harm as well as help you. In later years, I preferred the gentle physical arts, such as yoga, Pilates and therapeutic massage. But I was still green about my treatment options. To paraphrase the cliché, "I was young and needed the body work."

After my first chiropractor-induced bout of spinal weakness, I went to the government insured (OHIP) side of a local physiotherapy clinic. Months earlier, it had done wonders for my sub-patellar knee pain by administering ultrasound and ice and teaching me helpful straight-leg-raising exercises. However, my back problems were less straightforward than the knee problems had been. I'll never forget that young physiotherapy trainee Artur, a fit-looking, if squat, macho type, who looked me over, then sneered, "Yore bahk eez flat."

What followed were exercises in which Artur had me twist into a variety of pretzel shapes, to put a curve in my spine and presumably make more room for what he became convinced *must* be a protruding disk. (He was not impressed by all the negative x-rays.) At one point, feeling despondent, I asked Artur if he thought my problems would last months. He shook his head, very slowly, and intoned, "Eet weel take yeers ..."

Artur's more extreme exercises began to generate "chiropractor anxiety," but I persisted anyway, because that is what one *did* as a patient, especially a patient having gone to medical school himself. Artur's treatments were no walk in the park, but inspired my first rule about seeking help: *Look for someone who is sympathetic to your plight and who respects your physical limits.*

At one point in my "protean" condition, neck problems equalled those in my low back. I accepted a referral to an elderly rheumatologist, a medical doctor this time, who had developed a special "Shape of Sleep" pillow designed to perfectly support the neck during rest. It came in two sizes. This affable, if eccentric *eminence gris* prescribed the smaller (female) pillow, which I tolerated until it seemed to cause as many problems as it solved. The same man also believed that weak lower abdominal muscles were the root of all low-back evils. He instructed me to do frequent sets of brutal sit-ups, a match for any that the hotshots at the local Y showed off with in my youth. That he was telling even elderly patients to attempt the same later struck me as preposterous, and led to my second rule: *Beware of one-size-fits-all or one-exercise-suits-all solutions.*

The pharmaceutical industry learned the lesson the hard way. Some people did not respond to the starting dose of a medication as expected, and their individualized dose might be a quarter of what most people needed. Recently, the industry has come up with two separate drugs they claim are geared to fibromyalgia, with the lyrical sounding names Cymbalta and Lyrica. However, the juries are still out, and there are still more adventures to recount from the alternative realm.

For a time I went for repeated shiatsu treatments by the Japanese practitioner who first brought this therapeutic art to Toronto. Shiatsu felt like a massage in spots that seemed highly unlikely, until I consulted a map of energy meridians. It gave a sweet pain that was not altogether unpleasant. The Shiatsu Centre's claim that it was "exchanging the blood" of patients was rationalized this way: causing tiny bruises in the microcirculation, was removing old blood from the circulatory system, which the body would have to replace. This, it was claimed, lowered the body's burden of toxins, many of which were stored in the fat cells. Nothing I had learned in physiology made me believe this was so, yet after shiatsu treatments, as after other forms of Swedish massage, I emerged in la-la land, more relaxed than I normally am, and generally in better spirits. How could that be a bad thing? Afterwards, I would walk long distances, wander into stores and make impulse purchases to celebrate my more effortless gait. However, by the next morning, lactic acid would reassert itself and cause pains I had never gone in with. Yet, overall, I felt a net gain in my flexibility – and isn't preserving flexibility what therapy of any kind is all about?

I did experience the ministrations of an ur-therapist. Linda (alternative therapists often prefer to be called by their first names and usually call you by yours) was a physiotherapist at the Clinic of Injury and Disease Response (CIDR), who drove in from Oakville to see her patients in Toronto. Linda had a formidable armamentarium of skills, and depending on my entrance complaints, could perform cranio-sacral manipulations, massage and even acupuncture. At one point, she referred me for a procedure called dry needling, in which real needles, with a larger bore than the hair-thin needles of acupuncture, were inserted into the active muscle trigger points. A medical doctor did the honours, although I understand physiotherapists commonly perform such treatment these days.

While dry needling was helpful, it hurt like hell. Nearing fifty at the time, I worried about having a heart attack on the examining table. However, Dr. Heather offered to shoot the areas about to be needled with a laser gun to make the procedure more tolerable. I recall that my late mother would get terrible joint pains, for which she would have shots of cortisone into her shoulder bursa. Perhaps shots of saline would have worked as well, or even just inserting the needles themselves into the zone of intense pain, dry-needling style – but how could she have known?

Linda accepted my body as it was and worked one-on-one to improve it. Perhaps, as a physician, I got the VIP treatment. I never felt rushed out of her office. She also imparted new exercises I could do on my own and useful meditation skills. But alas, she decided the trek from Oakville was too expensive, and once again I was left to my own devices.

One of the many suggestions Linda made was that I be fitted with orthotics. I had heard about a podiatrist who attributed such poorly understood phenomena as "piriformis syndrome" to an improperly aligned gait and poor posture, both of which I have in spades. Nevertheless, as I sat in a dingy, packed waiting room, a veteran of too many treatments, I doubted that orthotics would really help my numb, cold and painful feet. "Here," said Dr. Glen, tapping my ankle bone (what in medical school we called the medial malleolus), "does this reproduce your symptoms?"

As he tapped away, my symptoms did indeed intensify, and I readily shelled out several hundred dollars for a pair of inside and outside orthotics. By the time I adapted to using them, my feet symptoms had improved by about 20%. If only every round of alternative medicine treatments were that successful.

Only within the past year have I discovered that chronic myofascial pain has several quite specific treatments, with which most medical and complementary therapists are not familiar. The following list also comes from the National Fibromyalgia Partnership's brochure *Myofascial Pain Due to Trigger Points:*

- Manual trigger point therapy.
- Metatarsophalangeal (MTP) injections with stretching.
- Spray and stretch therapy with vapocoolants or ice stroking.
- Galvanic stimulation.
- Microstimulation.
- Specific frequency microcurrent.

There is a scientific, perhaps pseudo-scientific ring to such treatments. Many alternative medicine therapists can offer one or more, but first they need to get the diagnosis right. For those with limited funds who can afford only a few sessions, or those who have difficulty speaking English at clinics lacking multilingual outreach, the above wish list is impossible to convey, let alone have fulfilled. At the present time, there are few publicly funded ways of accessing such treatments – a shame, given how much early intervention can limit future physical deterioration. I have heard about only one rheumatologist in the city of Toronto who offers these treatments.

Recently, a cottage friend introduced me to Pilates exercises designed to strengthen the abdominal core of the body. The exercises vary in difficulty, and may be scaled back as "restorative Pilates" for those who cannot perform at the higher level. The problem, at least for a man who finds dance steps complicated, is that its many highly refined, nit-picky exercises take time to master. At ninety dollars per hour, it is discouraging to leave the therapist's office with exercises difficult to reproduce at home and too easy to get wrong. However, an assertive client can ask the instructor write down everything, including how and when to breathe. To me, Pilates represents the height of useful active, as opposed to passive, methods to regain or retain strength and flexibility. Also, it seems less dicey than mechanical weights, since a long affair with a cross-country ski machine, while in posture misalignment, brought on my muscle problems in the first place.

For now, those on the cusp of developing these disorders should accept the good advice common to both family therapists and alternate medicine practitioners:

- Eat healthily.
- Exercise as much and as sensibly as you can.
- Get proper sleep – even if you require medication to do so. Recent new medications found helpful for both fibromyalgia and mysofascial pain include Cymbalta and Lyrica, though both are licensed for routine use in the US, but not yet Canada. I blush to add that cannabinoids may also be useful for these pain conditions, but would hate to think of their effects on the cognitive blurring known as "fibro-fog" that often accompanies these conditions.
- Take frequent breaks from sedentary work, paying special attention to ergonomics, posture and body awareness.
- Take generous supplements of Vitamin D since low levels of that vitamin may cause what the medical profession calls

Chronic Widespread Pain (CWP) that affects about 10% of the general population.

- Maintain healthy relationships.
- Consider some form of psychotherapy if your pain begins to affect your mood and exhaust the patience of family and friends.

Focal cognitive therapy and mindfulness meditation can help reduce catastrophizing, ruminating behaviour and pain-centred behaviour that allow physical symptoms to dominate your mental life. They are useful adjuncts to physical treatments and may well reduce the necessity for them. Some hospitals have pain clinics for those most in need, although the therapies provided in the general community are too rarely covered by provincial medical plans.

There is strong evidence for the therapeutic benefits of education about these conditions, aerobic exercise (hooray for walking and Pilates) and cognitive behavioural therapy for helping sufferers soldier on with their usual life activities and regain the benefits of improved sleep. There is also strong evidence for the two newer medications mentioned earlier, with Cymbalta (duloxetine) working best when there is accompanying depression and Lyrica (pregabalin) being particularly helpful in improving sleep. However, since drug companies contributed money to the research of some of the speakers at the American College of Rheumatology Annual Meeting, readers may wish to remain sceptical of these always-tentative drug claims.

Sadly, as of this writing (at least if you believe those too-often unempathic men and women in the white coats), there is only weak evidence for the benefits of acupuncture, chiropractic, massage therapy, electrotherapy and ultrasound.

Above all, patients should not let these alternative treatments bankrupt them or allow anyone too zealous about their unique approach to make them worse.

Now, if I could just leave behind my dual, sedentary professions, the computer and the car, surely long contemplative walks by the lake, Walden-style, would ease my blockages and redistribute my qi.

However, like hunching far too long before a computer screen, one can spend inordinate amounts of time positively *catering* to one's body and, in the process, accidentally become like one of the pampered characters in Steve Martin's comic movie *L.A. Story.*

While I prefer not to be a physical wreck, I acknowledge that to some, a "physical culturalist" is also a valetudinarian and, to the unsympathetic, just another variety of hypochondriac. (The word comes from the Greek words "hypo" and "chondrium" – loosely translated as "beneath and below the ribs"; presumably hypochondriacs worry about the organs situated there.)

In the end, what may keep us healthy is the ability to remain optimistic. Between her recurring seasonal depressions, my mother would go for cortisone shots for painful bursitis in her shoulders. She had arthritis, but may also have had fibromyalgia, or a chronic pain disorder. She would always tell her sons, "It's a great life," but added, "if you don't weaken."

"So, Why Do You Write?"

The poem and the consulting room

The question was asked by a friend, who, like me, is in her fifties, and who, by any measure other than financial, is a highly successful, award-winning poet. We were on a ravine walk on the kind of wistfully mild, early autumn afternoon that stirs ruminations on the meaning of life.

"Why not ask what makes me tick?" I thought, but, instead, countered with, "Can I have an hour to answer?" I proceeded to do so, as best as I could. It reminded me of that dreaded question medical trainees are asked when they go to their first interview for a residency position in psychiatry: "So, what made you choose psychiatry?"

Ah, psychological determinism. Why, indeed? There are dozens of levels at which one can answer such a question, but some might prove more detrimental than others to one's chances of being admitted to a psychiatry program. Most applicants realize this, and offer answers at the 50% candour level, answers like, "Even as a child, friends would come to me with their problems" to "I had a favourite aunt who was very 'colourful' when I was young." However, one could shoot the moon, and say, ". . . as was my mother," or even, "I had a period of depression (or anxiety) myself when I hit adolescence, saw a therapist, and never looked back . . . or rather, I did look back – a lot – and it really helped."

When asked to write a blog for the New York University's medical humanities website on my dual calling, I submitted the following:

A Psychiatrist and a Poet

> To be both a psychiatrist and a poet is either a dual calling or a double whammy, depending on what you choose to emphasize. Such a medical/literary hybrid has surely won the sweepstakes in the personal sensitivity department. I am often asked whether being a psychiatrist helps me to be a better poet, though few

people ask the reverse question, especially since I don't do "poetry therapy" in my psychotherapy practice. Before answering, a little more wordplay on the dual title may be in order.

One raises fewer eyebrows if one says "I'm a psychiatrist who also writes poetry" than, "I'm a poet who does psychiatry on the side." The obvious difference in job security and monetary status of the two activities might lead to offbeat explanations like, "I couldn't make a living as a psychiatrist, so I went into poetry for the money" or "Poetry is my day job, but I do psychiatry out of love."

There haven't been many psychiatrists/poets writing in English, at least not to the point of publishing (as opposed to self-publishing) several books. In the United States, people like Richard Berlin and Ronald Pies come to my mind. A few others are represented in the anthologies of world physician poetry, *Blood and Bone* and *Primary Care,* published by the University of Iowa Press.

The late, great American poet Robert Lowell had a psychiatrist – or, actually, he had ample cause to visit *his mother's* psychiatrist, Merrill Moore – a man who penned verse in what he nicknamed his "sonnetarium" at the back of his New England home. In other languages, Sweden's Tomas Transtromer, who had a psychology background, saw patients and specialized in writing about people on the brink of doing something truly desperate, or at least, transformative.

I started writing in earnest in pre-adolescence, and entered many essay and poetry-writing competitions, usually getting an honourable mention or placing second or third, which only whet my appetite to try harder. After being a psychiatrist for the past twenty-seven years and a psychotherapist for the past thirty, I would say that practicing the craft has given me a good ear for dialogue and monologue, for how people actually talk and think. Dream analysis has also sensitized me to the value of using dreams as bridges to more fully understanding people's fears, preoccupations and goals.

Psychiatrists from the past whose work informs my own include Freud, whose main prize, the Goethe Prize, was in literature, not medicine, and the late

Heinz Kohut, whose nearly unreadable books nevertheless are rich in their appreciation of the powers of the literary imagination and very rich indeed in their conception of the needs of a viable self. I also pay heed to the advice of more prosaic, left-brain theorists like Aaron Beck, who invented cognitive therapy.

Being a poet informs my work as a psychiatrist insofar as both callings focus intensely on language and its many layers of meaning. The mind is hard-wired to make and to understand metaphor, something the neuroanatomists have only begun to study. Many of my poems are about medicine in general and psychotherapy in particular, and I would refer the reader to rather amusing if vaguely unsettling pieces on such procedures as "MRI" and "Colonoscopy," both poems written from the perspective of the wary physician/patient who "knows too much."

I would offer a caveat for those who want to join me in the dual calling. Being a psychotherapist is especially hard on the back, given the relatively fixed postures one must sit in for large portions of the working day. Being a writer can also be hard on the back; ask Philip Roth who often works at a stand-up desk. Poets, of course, have it easier than novelists, but the physical issues add another form of double jeopardy to the work.

Psychiatrists and psychoanalysts are often talent *manqués* (missed talents), men and women who rarely emerge from behind their therapeutic neutrality. They get few opportunities to assert themselves as people with strong opinions and viewpoints, at least not in the consulting room, where to do so might be inappropriate. However, I work a lot with adolescents, who have "automatic shit detectors" and who appreciate frankness and, above all, engagement. Knowing I am a poet, other physicians often send me referrals who are actors, screenplay writers, even the occasional poet.

The patients in my poems are composite creations, but actual patients serve as springboards for fictional portraits that may include autobiographical takes on myself and my family. It might sound overly cautious, if not downright paranoid to state, at the end of a book of poetry which everyone knows to be a work of fiction,

> "No character in this book is identical to any living person," but I am tempted to do exactly that. In the end, I find the first-person-singular voice to be very effective and collar-grabbing and am usually willing to run the risk of the reader's deciding that the views presented in the poem are identical to that of its creator. Consider it the third hazard of this unique double calling.

I didn't have this blog material handy on the ravine walk with my friend, but she is a candid, serious person that always makes me strain for authenticity. "I was always writing, from early childhood. I kept submitting essays to competitions, always placing second or third, but that just made me try harder next time. So, competition had something to do with it."

"But what drove the competition?" she asked, taking me aback with her intuitive interviewing skills.

"There was a need for more power. My father was just five-foot-six, but weighed more than two hundred pounds. He would lord his bulk over me. He disapproved of my intelligence, my 'big mouth,' which only reminded him that he was less intelligent than his wife. I was the apple of her eye, and likely the mouthpiece for truths she might have said, had she not known better. Anyway, a sense of justice and fairness certainly drove me to write, still does, whether it's opinion pieces or the more emotional outpourings that turn into poems. And, I agree with you that the choice of poetry, given its obscurity and lack of an audience, doesn't make it easier to keep writing. I guess I've had my outlets in essays, though, *and* all those damn letters to the editor ... After all, if you feel the need to say something too personal to have anyone read, just tuck it inside a poem."

This struck a chord with my friend, who, despite several awards and much praise from critics, still struggles with doubts about each and every book she writes. She is painfully aware of the degree to which the general public overlooks them. I pressed on. "How does the old joke go: Publishing a new book of poems is like throwing a rose petal into the Grand Canyon and then listening for the echo."

"But look," she said, "You're a psychiatrist. I know a couple of psychiatrists, and *they* don't write."

"Hmmm ... You know, one of the main tools of my psychiatry trade is empathy. Perhaps the ability to feel along with others inclines me to both professions. It's hard to treat someone in psychotherapy if you can't experience how they might feel. But that means extending yourself in a certain way, in order to be fully present with them in the 'holding environment' of the session.

"If I can't achieve that with, say, someone with florid schizophrenia, or someone who is a dangerous bigot or a misogynist, then maybe I ought to avoid trying to treat those kinds of people, (though I hear Aaron Beck saying in the back of my mind, 'Aren't those just labels?')

"I mean, I feel a lot for humans, but don't get very worked up over the plight of, say, slaughtered animals; so I don't end up writing books that advocate animal rights."

"So," she said, "you write about what you identify with?"

"Yes, though great writers, of course, empathize with everyone and everything in their story, heroes and villains alike," I said, thinking of the most recent novel I had read, Alaa Al Aswany's novel, *The Yacoubian Building.*

"Does dealing with the kinds of emotional problems you see keep inspiring you to write?"

"I had heard Salman Akhtar, a psychoanalyst and Urdu poet, joke that writing a poem was like a person doing psychoanalysis on herself, while a therapist and a patient working together were like two people trying to write a poem. He also said that a poem resembles a beautiful neurotic symptom, while a neurotic symptom is like an ugly poem."

"Did he say that tongue-in-cheek?"

"Well, there are things that poems and neurotic symptoms have in common. Like motivations from early childhood, a certain impulse that triggers them and a kind of wish fulfilment for wrongs done to the author. That's straight out of Freud's *Creative Writers and Day-dreaming.* But Akhtar pointed out the differences between the two."

"Such as ..."

"Well, for one, poems are much more entertaining than neurotic symptoms. They can be shared to the benefit of others and they lead to better understanding of some aspect of self. Actually, he wrote an engaging short essay which he called 'A Bit of Prose about Poetry,' in which he describes ten functions of a poem, and he considers the essay a poem, partly because he wrote it in a single sitting, in just forty five minutes."

"Are you hiding behind your references?"

"I doubt it. I'm more an inspirational writer than a scholar. References are not my strong point."

"So, is there anything about doing the kind of work you do that makes you write, and poems in particular?"

"Maybe it has to do with time. Poems are the only thing I have *time* to write. Oh, and an essay or two ... But aren't you *really* asking yourself why *you* keep plugging away at it – though I've noticed you're also drifting towards prose?"

On that shrinky note, we decided to leave the matter, because it was autumn, the sun was setting, the temperature falling and an orange-red glow began to spread across the bowl of the ravine, like the afterglow of an excellent poem or perhaps a shadow play.

Down in the Dark: Poetry in Psychiatry

(*Poetry Canada Review,* Summer, 1990)

There is, and perhaps always will be, a healthy amount of suspicion, even competition, between poets and psychological healers. After all, the two professions both strive to understand the psyche and achieve an expertise in the full range of human emotions. As a poet who happens to be a psychiatrist, I often find myself in the role of trying to demystify the beliefs and practices of one of these two groups to the other. It's not usually an easy task.

For example, after I sent in the first draft of this article to *Poetry Canada Review,* I got back this reply from then-editor Maggie Helwig:

> Your article is interesting, but I don't think I can use it in its present form ... First of all, it bogs down too much in psych-jargon, to which I have a great aversion. It is probably the main thing that turns people against therapists – that they speak in this disempowering language that only other therapists really understand. You should also keep in mind that most writers are fully aware of the destabilizing and destructive aspects of their profession and quite willing to choose to pay the cost, even if it means a few brilliant poems and suicide. That very often is a conscious decision and should be respected as such, even if one believes that it is ultimately, in some way, wrong. You must go down into the dark, and sometimes nothing – not therapy, not religion – can bring you out the other side ...

I found Helwig's suggestion that I rework the article somewhat chastening; after all, I thought I'd managed to set out my views in acceptably plain English (though on re-reading my article I came to see her point). Her reply, concise and eloquent as it is, helped me to crystallize my own thinking, in that it neatly summarized the kind of arguments one often hears from writers when the subject of creative writing and mental illness is broached.

In the first version of this essay I put forth some reasons why the writing of modern poetry can in itself be stressful. How, for example, poetry has become, over the past thirty years or so, more and more confessional in nature, and more and more fragmented (the recent movement back to formalism notwithstanding). It is easy to speculate that the intensely personal material which, say, confessional poets were working with might well have served to intensify their mood swings, or increased their sensitivity to their poems being rejected – as if they themselves, or parts of themselves, were being rejected. And that such dynamics might have contributed to the high rates of suicide and madness among poets like Sylvia Plath, Robert Lowell, Anne Sexton, Randall Jarrell, John Berryman and Theodore Roethke. Nor could the balancing act these poets had to perform, between self-disclosure and bad taste, have been made any easier by the fact that the art form they chose paid so poorly in both money and reputation, and was read by a relatively small percentage of the reading public.

But even as I presented such material about what one might call "the perils of writing modern poetry," I hastened to add that it may not be such "occupational hazards" per se that bring the modern poet to a premature death, so much as the poet's behavioural responses to those stresses. And I wondered aloud how long the casualty list would have been, even among American confessionals, had the variable of alcohol abuse been factored out.

More and more, as a practising psychiatrist who sees a lot of creative young people, I'm coming to believe that it's not so much that any one type of creative activity is uniquely stressful, but that there is a self-selected group of people who are attracted to the activity in question; and that perhaps a profession like the writing of poems attracts more than its share of inherently moody people.

Some recent research findings are beginning to point in this direction. For example, the University of Iowa's renowned psychiatric researcher Nancy Andreasen (who has a background in English literature as well as psychiatry) has been studying a group of thirty American writers on faculty at the prestigious University of Iowa's Writers Workshop over a fifteen year period. She has been finding that an unusually high percentage of the writers – some 80% of them – were treated for some sort of mood-related disorder. This has been in marked contrast to her comparison group – which was also made up of high achievers, and matched for age, education, social status and the like, of whom 'only' 30% showed similar psychopathology. (Her comparison group was also a rather "driven" group of very high achievers, which may account for their surplus of, say, manic-depressive illness, a condition in which high levels of pathology and high levels of ability and achievement often coexist.)

Of Andreasen's creative writers, 43% were thought to have some degree of manic-depressive illness. This is all the more likely to be a valid finding, insofar as it was *not* something Andreasen and her group had predicted in advance. Rather, they had expected to find an increased level of schizophrenia in the creative group, and not manic-depressive illness. Alcoholism, a condition now thought to be closely associated with manic-depressive illness, afflicted a whopping 30% of the writers, compared to 7% of the control group (and probably 4 to 5% of the general population). Most compellingly, during the course of the study, two out of the thirty creative writers had already committed suicide. Though the small sample size makes this figure not statistically significant, it certainly points to just how dangerous these conditions of disordered mood tend to be.

Andreasen has also looked for evidence of both psychopathology and creativity in the families of creative individuals. She has found an increase in both factors in the family members, with several of the same individual relatives, especially siblings of creative people, having both clinical psychopathology and high levels of creativity. Andreasen's findings lend added weight to those of a 1983 investigation conducted by American psychologist Kay Jamison. She surveyed forty-seven of the top British artists and writers and found that 38% of them had sought treatment for mood disorder, a rate about ten times that of the general population. Intriguingly, poets topped the list, some 50% of them reporting psychiatric intervention. Equally intriguingly, the rate for biographers, those writers whose work is perhaps furthest removed from creative fire, was lowest, though still about 20%. By further contrast, the rate for visual artists was about 13% – again, compared to 4 or 5% of the general population.

Coming at things from the very specialized base of an investigator in mood disorders, the University of Tennessee's Dr. Hagop Akiskal looked over his records of seven hundred and fifty patients, a much larger sample size, who were diagnosed as suffering from depression, manic-depression or schizophrenia, to see if any subgroup of these patients showed differing levels of creativity compared to normative samples. Interestingly, he found that those with severe manic-depression had high rates of being arrested for antisocial behaviours, but did not show a marked increase in creative achievements. But, among those with moderate versions of the illness (which Akiskal views as a kind of *forme fruste* or partial expression of the condition), fully 10% were artists and creative writers.

It is impossible in an essay of limited scope to do justice to what these findings might mean. To me as a poet, I'm not surprised that conditions characterized by extremely powerful feelings tend to occur often in people who write poetry, since poetry, perhaps more than most forms of writing, tends to get "written with the nerves"; in fact, it is hard to imagine someone writing an effective poem about anything he or she didn't have very strong feelings about. In that light, perhaps we ought to be more surprised that while 43% of Andreasen's sample were treated for mood-related disorders, more than half the writers needed no such treatment.

I'm certainly not surprised, as a psychiatrist, to hear (in Akiskal's work) that severe forms of manic-depression (those forms in which the individual is prone to losing touch with reality) are not very compatible with high levels of creative achievement. To me it's always been a wonder that a man as rocked by emotional disorder as Robert Lowell was, who had to be repeatedly hospitalized, who was prone to violent, assaultive rages, and who at times lost complete sense of his own identity and imagined himself to be a figure from the past nevertheless managed to leave behind a sizable body of great work, teeming with the most lucid truths. Surely such accomplishment is a testimony to the ability of manic-depressive disorders to remit, and to allow the sufferer complete returns to his premorbid state – a luxury that schizophrenia rarely allows its victims. (In the psychiatric profession there are examples of men who suffered from devastating bouts of manic-depressive illness, but who pulled together, and, while in more lucid states, pressed for reforms in the ways that psychiatry and society treat mentally ill patients. Such men included the American Clifford Beers, founder of the then-progressive mental hygiene movement and author of *A Mind That Found Itself*, and Toronto's influential C. M. Hincks, after whom a major treatment centre for adolescents is named.)

Anyone who reads books like Ronald Fieve's *Moodswing* or Anthony Storr's *Solitude* will come upon example after example of individuals with some variant of moodswings severe enough to be regarded as manic-depressive, who made major contributions to the world and, especially, to the literary world. Truly, manic-depressive illness, especially in its milder forms, or when it is counter-balanced by unusual bravery and determination to function on the part of the sufferer, can be a blessing to society as a whole, as much as it can be a curse to the individuals who suffer from it.

But to come back to a point made earlier. It's not simply having intense moods that determine whether you rise to the top of a given field or sink to the bottom of humanity, any more than inheriting certain creative abilities will prove sufficient motivation for launching a creative career. Rather, it's the individual's *responses* to her or his emotionality that make the difference. These responses are based on such things as how well their personality has developed, how able they are to be intimate with others or at least to have close acquaintances, the extent to which they are able to forgive their own imperfections and the extent to which they have developed a conscience. These are the kinds of differences that so often tip the balance towards living a creative life, versus "going along with" the forces of illness, and choosing the fast lane to an early death.

Too many poets who suffered from powerful mood swings chose to self-medicate with alcohol while many around them kept silent about their obvious self-destructiveness; or accepted these out-of-control behaviours as a necessary accompaniment to the creative process itself, part of what Helwig refers to as "going down into the dark."

Perhaps some people are condemned to inevitably go under, at a tragically early age. But it would be pessimistic of us, even cynical, to fail to reach out to help those who can very much be helped, instead of excusing, joking about or even glorifying their self-destructiveness. Manic-depressive or depressive illness, for example, and alcoholism are, for the most part, treatable or at least mitigatable conditions. But they all take a lot of united effort on the part of those who know the sufferer; it is better to warmly but firmly *confront* people who are heading for suicide, than it is to over-attribute intentionality and "conscious" decision-making powers to them, since they are usually truly desperate.

I dearly wish that Sylvia Plath's family doctor would have succeeded in having her temporarily hospitalized before she completed her suicide. Not just for the sake of her young children, but for the sake of all the unwritten poems she still had in her. Regaining her psychic equilibrium would have allowed her to add much more to the literary canon, poems that might have been of the quality of the ones she wrote before the fateful winter of 1963, during which her work deteriorated into fragmented raging. To those who would say, "Well, then, we would have missed out on those winter poems," I can only say that Plath would have written them from her hospital room, just the way that she wrote the poem "Tulips" a year earlier.

Not that I think that getting professional help is the only route for someone with a mood disorder to take. As a reader of literary biography, I am constantly impressed by how resourceful some literary figures have been at finding ways of soothing their tormented souls, and staving off self-destructive impulses which might have done in others with less resourcefulness. Contentious and extremely anxious individuals like T. S. Eliot or Robert Frost were able, time and time again, to rise above their nervous temperaments, and find support and soothing in institutions ranging from stable marriages (a first unstable marriage was almost Eliot's undoing), idealized mentor figures (such as the lifelong support and encouragement Eliot received from Pound), the Catholic Church or the world of nature (one thinks of Frost again, his efforts as a farmer, and his tendency to anchor himself to the world views of other older, more successful Yankee farmers, from whom he borrowed many of his best sayings).

But again, Eliot and Frost were essentially non-drinkers. When, in the reading of literary biographies of poets, one finds a lack of stabilizing institutions, and a turn instead towards destabilizing soothers like alcohol or drugs, the result for the individuals and their families is almost always tragic. Now and then, one reads about poets whose inherited emotional syndromes were too severe for them to even think of going without professional medical help, the latter providing them with varying degrees of temporary relief from their torment; one thinks again of Plath and Sexton, whose therapists did much to encourage their writing efforts; or of Robert Lowell, for whom the newly invented mood-stabilizing medication lithium was only available during the last three years of his life.

Finally, I am well aware that some poets fear that professional treatment of their emotional torment might in some way compromise their creativity – that the cure might be worse than the disease. In my experience, by the time the poet decides, or her or his family decides, that she or he is in urgent need of professional help, the point has already been reached when their symptoms have compromised or retarded their creative output. By that point, the person is too slowed down or sped up to really concentrate on their work; they are usually aware of having crossed over the line of addiction to some substance or other, or they have incurred enough senseless financial or emotional debts as to have caused their families and loved ones to move gradually away from them. They are often isolated, feeling helpless, even while refusing help and contemplating suicide.

It goes without saying that it is far easier to try and help such a person before this point is reached – perhaps at a time when their family and friends see the warning signs, even if the poet himself is still rationalizing his self-destructiveness under such bad-faith labels as "the tormented poet." To me such a label is more objectionable than a psychiatric one, because it never seems to be linked to a plan of positive action.

Poets on Prozac: Mental Illness, Treatment and the Creative Process

If the book *Poets on Prozac: Mental Illness, Treatment and the Creative Process,* edited by psychiatrist/poet Richard Berlin, were published in the United Kingdom, Canada or Australia, it might have been called "Poets in Therapy," a more accurate, if less sexy and alliterative title. About more than pharmacotherapy, the book casts light on the reservations many creative people have about getting help, with first-person testimonials from successful poets who found themselves in desperate straits.

In the words of the poet J. D. Smith: "For a poet, seeking treatment for depression is to break with an implicit social contract. To the extent that the culture at large has a view of poets, beyond acknowledging their existence as a strange but seldom seen life form, such as a platypus or giant squid, that view is based on the Romantic myth of the poet as a distraught creature, preferably consumptive, who occasionally breaks forth in a song or a dirge. The poet in this view is morose so that others do not have to be, a pack mule for the collective burden of consciousness."

When such reluctant individuals do seek professional help, the American health care system further complicates the matter with a scarcity of treatment resources, insurance company limitations and prejudices and out-of-pocket payments that poorly-paid creative artists can ill afford. Ironically, the first essay in the book by Welsh poet Gwyneth Lewis, expresses gratitude for the National Health Service that provided her with some fifteen years of weekly psychotherapy. Such contrasts to the American system were rightly debated during the recent presidential election campaign.

Many books have been written about the so-called confessional poets, such as Robert Lowell, Sylvia Plath and Anne Sexton, all of whom suffered bouts of extreme mental illness and whose creative writing careers, and very lives, were extended by psychiatric treatment. There have also been first-person narratives of mental torment written by masters of prose, such as novelist William Styron's wrenching account *Darkness Visible.*

The poets/patients who have provided Dr. Berlin with frank and revealing details of their illnesses have not achieved the mythic status of Lowell or Plath, or the fame of Styron. The nitty-gritty details of their struggle to keep writing despite a range of psychiatric symptoms that includes mood swings, debilitating anxiety, eating disorders and post-partum depression will resonate with any creative person in need of relief yet simultaneously fearing the effects of becoming more stable or less exquisitely sensitive. In Gwyneth Lewis's words, "Since I was a child, I've lacked an emotional epidermis. This is good for writing – it means I can sense a lot – but bad for one's daily equilibrium."

Several of the poets offer excerpts from their work, including poems written both in medicated and unmedicated states. The issue of how medication affects creative writing can never be fully resolved, though Lewis states, "Even if it were proven that antidepressants adversely affected my ability as a poet, I'd still take them. After being a zombie for months, being able to write at all is a miracle, and that participation in the creative discipline, rather than a more objective measure of excellence, is the bottom line for me."

This book belongs on the shelves of all therapists who treat women and men who immerse themselves in creative writing or any other fine art. Dr. Berlin's pithy introduction provides a useful summary of the relationship between creativity and emotional disorder. The sixteen essays and the poetic excerpts that bolster them share the virtues of being heartfelt, accessible and brief. They can be read by all literate women and men, even those in the midst of an emotional maelstrom.

No less a psychiatrist than Freud wrote, "Everywhere I go I find that a poet has been there before me." No less a poet than the great American Robert Lowell wrote, after yet another debilitating round of bipolar illness, "Everyone's tired of my turmoil."

Section Three

Religion & Identity

Rise of Fundamentalism is Scary

"What's so scary about Muslims?"
Letter to the Editor
(*The Toronto Star,* December 5, 2007)

The answer to Yilmaz Alimoglu's question can be seen on the first page of the World section of the same-day *Toronto Star,* in which Afghan women are risking their lives for the privilege of the less-obstructed vision of the niqab relative to the utterly confining burqa.

There is something scary about all varieties of fundamentalism, and I doubt that Alimoglu, whose name has a Turkish ring to it, would disagree. The Turks are among the most Westernized and egalitarian of all Muslim nations and enjoy co-operative relations with Israel. Alimoglu's organization of Muslims and non-Muslims has the ring of social organizations that seek better relations between Christians and Jews or blacks and Jews.

A post-9/11 world that has featured subway and marketplace bombings and beheadings carried out by fanatics in the name of Islam is a world in which garments that conceal the body or the face are bound to cause discomfort among those not wearing such dress.

Is Alimoglu aware that there is a recurring wave of anti-Semitism in Europe that has been attributed to the rise of fundamentalism in certain isolated Muslim communities? Often the anti-Semitism is rationalized as an anti-Israel stance, but it stings those on the receiving end, especially when the threat of violence is involved.

Last summer I was driven to Ben Gurion airport by an Israeli cabbie who told me that whenever he visits his son in North America, he notices that Jews and Arabs get along better in the New World. He noted that Christian Palestinians have an affinity with secular Jews, because both sides are wary of fundamentalists.

May all the parties in Canada's growing ethnic mosaic find enough common ground to leave behind old dislikes and outright hatreds and accommodate to a new world in which full and equal rights of women are never again seen as negotiable, let alone reversible.

Fresh Thinking Needed on Mideast

Re: New Middle East plan urged,
Letter to the Editor
(*The Toronto Star*, November, 2008)

A new peace plan proposed by Giora Eiland, former head of Israel's National Security Council, will be dismissed as self-serving and an example of Israel's divide-and-conquer policy. It emphasizes the role of neighbouring states like Egypt and Jordan, involves land exchanges with Egypt and the recognition that Israel cannot possibly dislodge a popular social-military movement like Hamas from the Gaza Strip.

Those who push for a two-state solution have the best intentions, but may be engaging in self-deception. How is it possible to make peace and "live alongside" an enemy that has deep internal divisions (not dissimilar to those within Afghanistan or, for that matter, Pakistan) and that has adopted highly lethal practices like suicide bombing or rocketing cities?

The problem is really one of chaos, of "failed states" in which heavily armed warlords, family clans, bandits, kidnappers and a variety of religious zealots have firepower equal to that of government forces. The best way to deal with this situation may well be to have the armies of sovereign states move in and disarm splinter groups and civilians.

One problem, however, is that the international arms trade benefits from chaos and from all parties receiving weapons. This is why no one is speaking out against the wanton spread of weapons, and why the arms bazaars in Quetta, Pakistan, or the arms-smuggling tunnels of Gaza will remain open, so that weapons can keep moving. The export value of weapons to the developing world exceeds the value of exported car parts. In tough times, weapons are among America and Russia's more viable exports, even if they are caked over with human blood.

Comedian Chris Rock captured this absurdity when noting that the US wants to disarm Afghanistan, yet can't even disarm Baltimore.

Cowboy Nation

On the eve of the American election, John McCain's critics commented that America did not need another "cowboy president." Many saw the two-term president George W. Bush as a cowboy, albeit a Connecticut cowboy who caroused at Yale before becoming governor of Texas and holing up at a ranch in Crawford, Texas. In Dick Cheney, Bush certainly had a crusty cowboy oil-man on leave from a Wyoming ranch and straight out of central casting, at his side.

Writing in the oh-so-liberal *Huffington Post,* Phil Bronstein had this to say: "You have to admit, eight years away from his Wyoming ranch have not taken a single kerchief stitch of the cowboy out of Dick Cheney."

Cheney's the man who accidentally shot "an acquaintance" of thirty years in the face, and somehow the man ended up apologizing for the trouble he caused the vice-president. Trouble was also stirred by John McCain, who was "plain wrong" to insist that waterboarding was a form of torture. By the time McCain made his case, Cheney's icy stare and gravely voice had lost some of their power to strike terror into the hearts of government staffers.

Nor is Canada immune to the cowboy ethos. Prime Minister Stephen Harper is a native Ontarian transplanted to Calgary, where he morphed into a Westerner and revived a moribund Conservative Party. As I write this, Mr. Harper managed to get the Governor General to slap a lock on the House of Commons when it looked like his government might be brought down by a coalition of other parties. At his side is his deputy Stockwell Day, a public safety minister who, along with the country's justice minister Rob Nicholson, strongly disbelieves in the national firearms registry. Each year the three men conspire to offer amnesties to thousands of Canadian gun owners who either fail to register their weapons or to renew their licenses, thereby ensuring that the registry is less useful to the police chiefs across the country, who consult it daily.

There was also the mythic status of that other cowboy president, Ronald Reagan, who made Americans feel good about themselves again, and who escalated an arms race that nearly bankrupted the once-mighty Soviet Union. His actions spawned thousands more nuclear warheads that scientists still struggle to account for, any one of which could wind up in the wrong hands, but hey!, the Berlin Wall came down, even if another wall sprung up in the Holy Land. The old Soviet empire was whittled down to Russia and its satellites, even as the genial Gorbachev gave way to the clown-like Yeltsin and then the inscrutable KGB man, Vladimir Putin.

Under successive Republican administrations, the word "Liberal" might as well have been preceded by "bleeding-heart." A neo-conservative ethos dominated TV, cable TV and radio channels. One often heard the saying, "A Conservative is a Liberal who's been mugged by reality," but it was not until after the implications of the Patriot Act and Abu Ghraib prison sunk in that one heard the rejoinder: "A Liberal is a Conservative who has been arrested."

The McCain/Palin campaign abounded with pejorative uses of words like "liberal" and "socialist" and dire warnings about Barack Obama: "He is the most liberal senator on record." The wild west imagery continued, with McCain proudly branding himself as a "maverick" and Sarah Palin being celebrated as an Alaskan version of a cowgirl who could hunt deer from a helicopter, field dress a moose and discharge a fully automatic rifle on a firing range.

The Republican Party era displaced liberal, social/humanist values with the brash adulation of naked self-interest. This type of self-interest had been portrayed as a benign influence on society in the books of Ayn Rand, who was much admired by the Chairman of the Fed Alan Greenspan, and many other neo-conservatives. Greenspan saw himself as a practitioner of what Rand might call The Virtue of Selfishness, the very title of one of her books. Before he came to the helm at the Fed, a younger Greenspan had written papers on the need to abolish the institution and had advised a return to the gold standard. He came to be admired as a master manipulator who pushed to abolish such rules as the extent to which banks needed to have cash on hand to balance their leveraged investments. He advised Republican Presidents since Ronald Reagan that "the free market knows best," believed in "trickle-down economics" and accepted Ayn Rand's notion that financial institutions, left to their own devices, would manage risk well enough to protect the assets of their shareholders and clients.

But the great meltdown on Wall Street made the bankruptcy of this neo-conservative ideology clear. The Nobel Prize in economics was awarded to Paul Krugman, a Liberal American Jewish economist who staked his career on condemning Republican fiscal and trade policies. The same laissez-faire approach to financial markets has also been applied to environmental protection and set the stage for an out-of-control firearms industry that was spreading concealable, semi-automatic firearms among an increasingly fractious civilian public. This happened at a time when a faltering McCain/Palin presidential campaign irresponsibly sought to brand Barack Obama as "palling around with terrorists" and implied that, if elected, Obama would prove to be a "socialist" who would rob from "Joe the plumber," (presumably to give to Joe the slummer). Leaders have been shot at for less.

Both cowboys and liberals share the blame for the rise of corporate greed and the near-death experience of the world financial system. Liberals blame the cowboys; Bush, Cheney and Greenspan; who championed years of free-wheeling deregulation of the financial markets, encouraged unrealistically low interest rates, unconscionable degrees of bank leveraging and the emergence of complex investment vehicles called "derivatives." These last were devised by complex computer programs and seemed to transcend common sense, with proponents insisting that ever larger profits could be made without incurring greater levels of risk.

From their vantage point, or advantage point, Conservatives blamed the "bleeding hearts," and the very spirit of liberalism initiated by President Lyndon B. Johnson's The Great Society, during whose time such agencies like The Department of Housing and Urban Development (HUD) sprang up, with a mandate to eliminate poverty and racial injustice. As a result of their ethos, organizations like Ginnie Mae, Freddie Mac and Fannie Mae came to be, through which the American government became progressively more involved in managing mortgage debt. These organizations encouraged many Americans who really could not afford it to purchase homes as part of an expanded American Dream, often with low or even no down-payments, in the wilfully naive belief that home values could only rise.

The naive liberal ethos of expanded home ownership was compounded by the reckless cowboy ethos of deregulation, during which time nearly half of American homeowners were encouraged by their investment advisors to re-mortgage their homes, based on the newly inflated market value of those homes. Americans began to treat their homes like their personal ATMs. The lure of tax-deductible mortgage interest, a government policy viewed as extravagant in Europe and Canada, made acquiring the largest possible mortgage seem like the obvious thing to do. People borrowed to buy that SUV, third car, cottage or boat, or to finance ever costlier vacations; even their credit card debt got wrapped into some esoteric investment vehicle that was, unbelievably, wrapped up and marketed as yet another investment commodity.

And while the United States engaged in a free market paradigm that set the stage for tumbling markets, it also set the stage for its failure in the Middle East. An article in *The Globe and Mail* by Doug Sanders, called "Yes, 1989 was huge ... but it's 1979 we have to worry about," points to crucial errors in American Cold War decisions to back the likes of the Stalinesque Saddam Hussein, as well as the two billion dollar support package for bin Laden and his *mujahedeen* in Afghanistan as pivotal disasters in American foreign policy that greatly affect us today. What gives me pause, as a liberal, is the recognition that 1979 was before the advent of the cowboy president, Ronald Reagan. At the time, the president was Jimmy Carter; the secretary of state, Cyrus Vance and the secretary of defense, Harold Brown, the first scientist ever to hold that position. Again, the responsibility for American militarism, elevated to a fever pitch during the George W. Bush presidency, must be jointly owned by Democrats and Republicans.

Recently, Norman H. Olsen, a twenty-six-year veteran of the American foreign service, wrote "An inside story of how the US magnified Palestinian suffering" in which he criticized his country's tendency to sponsor elections, then to interfere in them and to become punitive when they don't go America's way. Olsen believes that concerted American backing for Fatah and its Israeli-supported strongman Mohammed Dahlan was a factor in pushing the Palestinian populace to voting for what they perceived as the less corrupt and less corruptible group, Hamas. This is reminiscent of the original American sin in the Middle East, the toppling of the socialist Mossadeq in favour of the dictatorial Shah of Iran, and the later failed attempt to encourage the election of a CIA puppet strongman, Iyad Allawi, as the president of an occupied Iraq.

Reading Naomi Klein's revealing and deeply disturbing essay in *Harper's Magazine* titled "Baghdad Year Zero" first made me aware that the pointless invasion of Iraq was carried out in a way that produced maximum shame and frustration in those invaded and occupied. Firing the Iraqi army, and failing to prevent the looting of precious artefacts from the Iraqi National Museum, even while the Americans were careful to defend oil fields and pipelines, all added insult to injury, as did the repeatedly callous comments made by Donald Rumsfeld, Bush's secretary of defense. The theft of some three hundred metric tonnes of powerful plastic explosives from under the Americans' noses and misdirection of thousands of Pentagon weapons grotesquely multiplied the misery in store for the Iraqi people, in much the same way that the sale of semi-automatic handguns in the US multiplies domestic gun injury.

Set against these realities was the prediction by Bush's neo-conservative advisers that Iraqis would react with lasting gratitude to their new liberators – a prediction as insensitive as the Russian government's arranging a Leningrad Symphony concert in South Ossetia immediately after wresting away the disputed territory from Georgia. Similarly, the Supreme Court's *District of Columbia v. Heller* decision was singularly cold-hearted, given it came when the United States was reeling from gun violence and set to embark on yet another, particularly contentious presidential election.

Most Americans today know about the toppling of Saddam Hussein but have no desire to explore how American support of that Stalinesque dictator emboldened him to wage a bloody eight year war against Iran, a war during which the ethos of martyrdom became entrenched in both countries.

Whenever I mention Mossadeq or the Iran/Iraq War to an Iranian émigré, it brings a sigh of relief, as if he or she feels recognized as coming from a much more complex place than the one portrayed by the media.

A recent front-page article in *Harper's,* called "Prosecuting Bush," addresses the need for a bipartisan body that can investigate particularly the repeated use of torture by the Bush administration, and its exporting of suspects to countries known to practice torture. Indeed, the newly appointed Chair of the US Senate Finance Committee, Chris Dodd, is charged with investigating what precipitated the need for the largest government bailout since the Great Depression – and could well amount to the financial industry's own truth and reconciliation commission.

Don't Call Me White

Referring to other people as "black" or "white" leads to black-and-white thinking, something that's not good for anyone. It is time we rethought the words that we use to describe ourselves and our fellow Torontonians. (*The Toronto Star*, August 21, 2005)

I am listed in the census as being of "Caucasian" race and am also said to be "white." I am therefore not going to be stopped and searched by the Toronto police if they change their policy of avoiding racial profiling and accept city counsellor Michael Thompson's recommendation that "black men" in certain locations be subjected to such searches.

What does it mean to be identified primarily as "Caucasian" or "Negroid," "white" or "black"? A little history of such scientific and folk terminology is in order.

The concept of a "Caucasian race" sprang from the Enlightenment's passion for classification and Romanticism's obsession with human morphology.

It was first proposed by the German scientist Johann Friedrich Blumenbach (1752-1840) and was based primarily on skull features, best exhibited by the Georgians, a people living in the Southern Caucasus.

The Caucasus held a strong attraction for Blumenbach and other contemporaries because of its (imagined) proximity to Mount Ararat – where, according to Biblical legend, Noah's Ark eventually landed after the Great Flood. Sound scientific so far?

Later, anthropologists expanded Blumenbach's classification, dividing the Caucasian race into Nordic, Alpine, Mediterranean, Baltic and smaller subdivisions. Nordicism, the belief that the blond Nordic division constitutes a "master race," was influential in Northern Europe and the United States during the early twentieth century, eventually becoming the official ideology of the Nazi state. It was used to justify eugenics programs and the persecution and extermination of so-called "inferior" races then living in Europe, such as Jews and the Roma.

Nevertheless, Caucasian is still used in the United States and Canada as the scientific term for white. It is even used by many anthropologists and geneticists to refer generically to people of European origin.

Perhaps, like Groucho Marx, I am wary of joining any club that would have me as a member, but I have long been uneasy about the misnomer white.

Unlike the term Caucasian, the sanitary word white is typically withheld from slightly more olive-toned peoples, such as Hispanics. The major linguistic scam of our age, perhaps of any age, and one of great obstacles to egalitarian thinking, is that people of the pseudo-scientifically dubbed Caucasian race are actually white. It is as nonsensical an assumption as viewing those of the Negroid race as "black," thinking of Orientals as "yellow" or North American aboriginals as "red." Any man who fancies himself to be white need only place his hand atop a plain white sheet of paper.

Here I am not being merely concrete. As a poet, I understand the efficiency of a colour-wheel metaphor for describing our fellow human beings. Yet, in our collective unconscious, words take on the heft of real things. Some metaphorical terms reinforce our natural tendency to "black-or-white" thinking, which cognitive psychology has exposed as a barrier to viewing the world, or one's self, objectively.

Just reflect on what we normally think of as white: goodness, purity, clean sheets, snow, enlightenment, spirituality ("the white light") and mother's milk – though anyone who has seen real mother's milk knows it to be yellowy or, at best, off-white. In stark contrast is what we think about black: evil (black heart), darkness, filth and depression (what Churchill called his "black dogs").

This Manichean way of thinking plays directly into the hands of white supremacists. It is no accident that the Ku Klux Klan chose lily-white as the colour of their fearsome, if ludicrous, cloaks and hoods.

One of the most mesmerizing poems of the modern era is "Death Fugue" by Holocaust poet Paul Celan. It begins with an image designed to disorient and disturb:

> Black milk of daybreak we drink it at sundown
> we drink it at noon in the morning we drink it at night
> we drink and drink it.

We are no more likely to imagine black milk than we are to imagine a filthy pure-white surface, even though a page of paper, if contaminated with, say, anthrax powder, would be exactly that.

None of this is to deny that anthropologists have identified several clearly distinct races.

The one to which I have been assigned is properly called "Caucasoid," even though I personally have never ventured near the mountains of the Caucasus.

Wikipedia's take on the Caucasoid category was far less exclusive than what the colour white brings to mind in the popular imagination: "Caucasoid describes humans primarily from Europe, the Middle East (Western Asia), North Africa, the Indian subcontinent and parts of Central Asia, and is one of the four traditional major races recognized by physical anthropologists."

What follows is equally dry and not likely to set anyone's nose out of joint: "The Caucasoid or white race is not defined by social opinions about 'whiteness,' which are a folk taxonomy, but are based upon the shared anatomical features of Western Eurasian humans. Caucasoids present the lowest degree of projection of the alveolar bones, which contain the teeth, and a notable prominence of the nasal region."

No Hitler-like dictator could successfully advocate mass extinction based on the need to rid the world of such subtle anatomical differences.

He would require more incendiary, moralistic terms such as "lily-white race" or "dark forces of evil." Such exaggerations facilitate the kind of black-or-white thinking that attributes goodness, wisdom and progress to a dominant group of a presumed superior colour, and evil, ignorance and backwardness to savages, be they black Moors (consider the ace-of-spades colour of the enslaved men holding up lamps in Baroque-era statues), "red men" or the "yellow peril."

I am hardly the first person to think about the implication of dividing humanity into blacks (or coloureds) and whites.

In his epilogue to 2002's *When Race Becomes Real: Black and White Writers Confront Their Personal Histories,* former Harvard Law School professor Derrick Bell writes, "The good news is that there are now a host of writers and a growing number of courses and workshops designed to enlighten white people as to the real benefits and the great cost of their property in whiteness."

Many of those engaged in this Herculean task are white, Bell notes, among them Noel Ignatiev, author of *How the Irish Became White* and a fellow at the W. E. B. Du Bois Institute.

Ignatiev writes, "In the interests of survival, Afro-Americans have always studied *whiteness* (emphasis mine). There is a long tradition among them that the white race is a peculiar sort of social formation, one that depends on its members' willingness to conform to the institutions and behaviour patterns that reproduce it. By the early 1900s ... it was becoming commonplace in the academy to speak of race, along with class and gender, as a social construct ..."

Does the author really mean "relative whiteness," "pallor" or "pinkness?" Note how even in such relatively enlightened writing by an academic, the rigidly contrasting colour descriptions of variously tinted human beings are never seriously questioned.

The Women's Movement has championed the elimination of sexist terminology that reinforces stereotypes and perpetuates social inequalities. Thus, the people capable of running large, wealthy corporations are not "chairmen" but, rather, "chairpersons" or simply "chairs." Those capable of delivering the mail are no longer "mailmen" but "mail carriers."

Although comedians have ridiculed such politically correct recasting of popular terminology, it remains a valuable aid in debunking popular, stereotypical language that unconsciously reinforces social inequalities.

Islam is often vilified in the popular press by being confused with Islamic fundamentalism. Yet a scene of Muslims at prayer is the very model of people of all shades worshipping together as they surrender to a force greater than their common humanity. In many a Catholic cathedral, one also sees a commingling of various skin colours that is in contrast to the more monochromatic congregations of religions based in northern parts of the world.

As a psychiatrist, and especially as a poet, I would debunk this canard of a term "white" and replace it with a more accurate term, such as Caucasoid or Caucasian.

How downright revolutionary for white people to recast themselves as pinks, a change at which most red-blooded, certainly red-necked, men would balk. Those blessed with the good fortune of being dubbed white are actually pink to tan in colour (though less so during the dead of winter). Most Caucasians reach the apogee of pure whiteness only after death. Even those paler, more Nordic types among us are not truly white, nor even are those who are albino, unless they are also severely anaemic or at death's door.

The term "black" has perhaps undergone more revolutionary changes than the more blithely accepted term "white."

The 1960s saw the rise of the Black Power movement, which made virtue out of necessity by substituting the black word for terms like Negro, which were freighted with an ugly history. The Black Power movement gave rise to the "black is beautiful" aesthetic and expanded peoples' views about how inclusive a thing beauty could be.

Eventually, the mouthful "African-American" substituted a geographical term (akin to Caucasian) for the black. In our own day, hip-hop music has resurrected the word "Nigga" for its own shock purposes, no doubt to the chagrin of older people of all colours. Hip-hop/gangsta rap's stereotyped portraits of young "black" males go to the heart of how they are misperceived.

As a writer, the last thing I want to advocate is linguistic censorship. But no man, woman or child should use the terms white, black, yellow or red to refer to themselves or others without recognizing the metaphorical stretch in such terminology and its detriment to achieving peace on Earth and goodwill among one's fellow human beings.

People fortunate enough to be dubbed white will not easily give up on so flattering and self-serving a description. Nor are they likely to be aware of how other races may see the relative lack of pigmentation as a telling omission on the part of the creator.

To an artist, black is the presence of all colours, while the white of canvas is akin to an absence of colour. To a physicist, a white surface reflects back all wavelengths, while a black one absorbs them and does not reflect, unless it is a shiny surface.

Not that these intricacies of colour affect our core propensity to see any colour other than our own as unusual. The Japanese and Cantonese terms for "foreigner" – *gaijin* and *gwai lo* (which can also be used to mean "white devil") – attest to this impulse of naming who is "ours" versus "not one of ours."

I was informed by a friend that when her son and his travelling companions stopped by an isolated village in Ghana, they were surrounded by little children who gleefully taunted them with a reverse of a typical white racist taunt – "White monkeys! White monkeys!"

Any sensitivity-training reading list on the hardships of being stereotyped by colour would have to include Ralph Ellison's novel *Invisible Man*, as electrifying now as it was when it first came out more than fifty years ago: "I am an invisible man. When they approach me they see only my surroundings, themselves or figments of their imagination – indeed, everything and anything except me."

One could proceed to John Howard Griffin's wrenching account of a man's experiment in changing his colour, recounted in *Black Like Me*. Dick Gregory's book *Nigger: An Autobiography* also makes for a fascinating period piece. For a recent treatment of the danger of using words with race connotations, one can read about the professor whose life falls apart after he is unfairly accused of using a racial slur in Philip Roth's *The Human Stain*.

All of these books remind us that, if we cannot abandon an absolutist colour-coding of human beings (remember South Africa's apartheid division into whites, blacks and coloureds?) we should at least become more conscious of how this linguistic scam perpetuates unconscious assumptions about our own and other racial groups.

As for the question of who Toronto's finest should stop and search, I would nominate young males of any race in neighbourhoods where violence has occurred who wear clothing that might conceal weapons.

I would opt for a bit of sexism and ageism over racism any day of the week, especially in the twenty-first century, when racism is once again looming as an explosive issue.

Afterword

A letter writer to *The Toronto Star* later challenged my remark about opting for a bit of sexism over racism, pointing to the equally insidious nature of the two.

In the weeks following the meteoric rise to prominence of Barack Obama, the colour words used to describe him could gain added valence when used in certain ways. In a Toronto Star letter titled, "Don't use 'black' as a noun," written in August 2008, reader Richard Barrett wrote:

> Your story says Barack Obama is "the first black ever to carry his party's hopes." I have a problem with the use of the word "black." Is he the first black *man*? First black *senator*? Black *person*? I've never seen a white person described as just "a white." White man, yes, but never just "a white."
>
> As a black man, I have often been reduced to just the sum of my parts. Yes I am black, but I am much more than that. Being referred to as a black doesn't cut it anymore.

I am not advocating policing the English language, and do not expect people to use mouthful terms like "African-American" or "Caucasian" instead of shorter, more convenient colour terms like black, brown or white. I once wrote a suite of poems about the plight of Canadian First Nations peoples, then referred to as "Indians," and titled it "More Bones for the Red Man." It is interesting how flagrantly inaccurate colour adjectives like red or yellow have gradually slid into disuse. I ask only that we think about how we use colour language to describe each another, and on that, I very much agree with Mr. Barrett.

The North American colour wheel is changing. Whereas "whites" once made up 83% of the population, they now account for 65% in the United States. Hispanics have gone from less than 5% to more than 15%

and Asians from less than 1.2% to more than 5%. The growth rate of minorities is roughly 32% for Hispanics, 30% for Asians, about 9% for blacks and but 2% for whites.

White supremacists are becoming an increasingly lonely lot, hell bent on a mission impossible. The swearing in of a biracial president, with truly African-American ancestors in Kenya as well as Caucasian ancestors from Kansas to Honolulu is a victory for the acceptance of complexity as the road to repairing a world damaged by the black-or-white hatred of Nazi Germany; Selma, Alabama; Rwanda and Darfur.

Canaries in the Mind-shaft

Remember the "good old days," when meltdowns had to do with nuclear reactors and bailouts with airplanes? Liberals blame the collapse of the world's financial system on Conservatives and Conservatives blame it on the bleeding-heart Liberals, but devotees of black-or-white, all-or-nothing thinking, such as confirmed anti-Semites, much prefer to blame it on The Jews. Goldman Sachs, Lehman Brothers ... They simply can't resist.

Yet, when Mr. Greenspan was grilled by the head of a House of Representatives oversight and government reform committee, the man doing the grilling was also a Jewish American, Congressman Henry Waxman. Clearly, Jews are not the monolithic group that anti-Semites like to portray. They want you to think Greenspan, Bernanke or George Soros when you think "Jewish," rather than of prominent non-Jews like Treasury Secretary Henry Paulson Jr.; Daniel Mudd, the former CEO of Fannie Mae or Merrill Lynch's extravagant CEO John Thain. They certainly don't want you to think of Jews as the likes of Harry Houdini, LA Dodgers' pitching great Sandy Koufax, Bob Dylan, Frank (Goldberg) Gehry or Henry Winkler, the actor who played The Fonz on the TV series *Happy Days.* They would rather the name Hank Greenberg be associated with a bankrupt global insurance company rather than a former baseball legend.

One valid point on which anti-Semites are fixated is this: among Jews, one of the recent groups to have been emancipated from centuries of oppression, there are indeed highly outspoken individuals. They value *chutzpah,* which loosely translates into English as "unapologetic audacity." If they take public stands on issues, it is partly a reaction to centuries of having been forced to remain silent. If they are determined to succeed professionally, it is because, for decades, there were *numerus clausus* restrictions on the number of Jews (and indeed other ethnics and races) admitted to university professional schools.

In a wider sense, many Americans have come to value *chutzpah.* America was, after all, formed by groups of persecuted immigrants who, like the Jews, escaped to a new and better world and, as such, there are parallels to be drawn between the strong personality features, the exuberance and occasional, social and national pushiness of both Jewish and gentile Americans. Such subtleties, though, are lost on anti-Semites.

The cultural value of *Tikkun Olam* (the need to repair the world) has long propelled many of the best and the brightest of Jewish men and women to both the left and right of political and economic issues. Jewish idealism binds its people to an ancient covenant and an ancient language, even while *chutzpah* often tempts individual Jews to rebel against their own tradition, and attempt to address the ills of the wider world. The far-left causes of international socialism and communism were embraced by progressive young Jews, although many became bitterly disappointed after the execution of the Rosenbergs and when 'Uncle' Joseph Stalin showed his true colours. Social activism was championed by Jewish union boosters like Saul Alinsky, credited by some as having invented the phrase "Think globally, act locally."

As pointed out by Lewis Hyde, in a chapter on usury in his book *The Gift,* the earliest Christians shared communistic values, and during medieval times, he writes: "the image of the Christian era would be the bleeding heart ... The image of the Middle Ages is the expanding heart, and the deviant is the 'hard-hearted man. He is usually taken to be a Jew, the only man in town who feels no self-consciousness in limiting his generosity."

Hyde does not intend to sound anti-Semitic. Rather, he is referring to the Old Testament laws of Moses in Deuteronomy that are indeed ambiguous about the practice of usury (what we would now call interest rates) and which allowed the Israelite tribe to treat loans differently within their own tribe versus loans to the strangers on the borders of their community. These usury laws were boldly challenged by Jesus, who overturned the money lenders' tables and insisted that all men be treated like brothers, a policy much easier to preach than to turn into workable economic policy.

Hyde's chillingly worded passage (chilling, at least, to Jews) is a reminder that the sense of European Christendom as a community was partly achieved through projecting selfishness and depravity onto a vilified other. Most often that other was the quintessential outsider, The Jew, and sometimes, as during the Crusades, The Muslim. It is ironic that, since 9/11, North American Muslims have had to endure suspicion and hostility of a kind formerly directed mainly at Jews. African-Americans, of course, could receive more negative projections should Obama misplay his presidential role, or perhaps, play it all too well.

Hyde continues his discussion of usury with a description of how, under Martin Luther, and later, men like John Calvin and philosopher Jeremy Bentham, the practice of charging interest on loans came to be seen as justified, even as vital to preserving the economic interest of society. While he discusses Luther's views on the Deuteronomy laws, he fails to mention that Luther became very anti-Semitic once it became clear that the Jews were not going to convert en masse to the newly created Protestant church.

Jews rarely support extreme-right causes, because fascists often use the hatred of Jews (or communists) to unite disparate groups behind populist slogans. However, the far American right was indeed galvanized by two modern Jewish thinkers aside from Ayn Rand. The first was a political philosopher from the University of Chicago named Leo Strauss. His philosophy was anti-liberal, and some read his views as condoning leaders to tell "noble lies" to their people, in the spirit of doing what they know to be best for them. The second, also from the University of Chicago, was economist Milton Friedman.

Friedman became the darling of neo-conservatives, who selectively read his books to justify government non-intervention in the economy. So extreme was Friedman's libertarianism that he advocated eliminating Social Security, minimum-wage laws, public housing, tariffs, subsidies, even government licensing requirements for professionals. For every Friedman, there is, of course, a more mainstream (as in less extreme) Jewish economist, like Paul A. Samuelson, also of the University of Chicago, whose theories are taught as widely as Friedman's, but were never taken up by the neo-conservatives.

The fact that most of the CEOs, bank managers and insurance company presidents are not Jewish, but Christian, does not make me feel less compelled to write about the Jewish ethnicity factor – especially when the American B'nai B'rith has to scramble to deal with highly inflammatory, sometimes frankly anti-Semitic videos on YouTube blaming the entire global financial crisis on the world's perennial scapegoat, the Jews.

A bottom line here is that anti-Semites use hatred of the relative success of Jews to maintain a sense of righteous indignation and of having been cheated. Like the Scots and the Irish, to give two examples, Jews have indeed been successful out of keeping with their modest numbers. Though they make up less than 0.02% of the world's population (roughly thirteen million people), they represent nearly 10% of the Forbes 400 list of the wealthiest people. They also account for a high percentage of Nobel Prize winners in such fields as mathematics, physics and chemistry, the product of a devotion to higher learning that underlines their reputation as "The people of The Book."

Here is a quote from the twelfth century Jewish sage Maimonides: "He who wishes to attain to human perfection, must therefore first study Logic, next the various branches of Mathematics in their proper order, then Physics and lastly Metaphysics."

Of course, the Jews are hardly alone in playing the role of the vilified other. Hyde points out elsewhere in *The Gift* that all cultures seem to find a slightly alien local population onto which to project the image of the mercantile swindler:

"For the Vietnamese it is the Chinese, and for the Chinese it is the Japanese. For the Hindu it is the Muslim; for the North Pacific tribes it was the Chinook; in Latin America and the American South it is the Yankee. In Uganda it is the East Indians and Pakistanis. In French Quebec it is the English. In Spain the Catalans are 'the Jews of Spain.' On Crete it is the Turks, and in Turkey it is the Armenians."

Indeed, the Irish are sometimes regarded as "the Jews of the UK," and have been vilified as dirty, superstitious and inordinately possessed of the gift of the gab.

The reader would do well, then, to see my selective focus on Jewish ethnicity as bespeaking my personal upbringing and my own efforts to deal with both my love of this people and simultaneous awareness of its historically precarious perch in the world. Whoever wrote the song "Don't Worry, Be Happy" probably was not Jewish.

As I write this, the Israeli army has re-entered Gaza, in response to repeated rocket fire on Israeli cities and towns by the Hamas. The resulting photos of injured and dying, dark-eyed Palestinian children, who poignantly resemble Israeli children, has drawn concern and harsh condemnation of Israel in many parts of the world. It has also caused a good deal of agonizing among Jews living both in and out of Israel who are also appalled by the carnage, even if the Israeli military blame it on the Hamas policy of setting up weapons caches in public places and shooting from areas packed with civilians.

The actions of Israel on the world stage, as the Jewish state responds to the tough neighbourhood in which it was created, inevitably contribute to the waxing and waning of anti-Semitic feeling. Even though Northern Israel has been harassed for eight years by Hamas rockets, even though suicide bombs killed, maimed or traumatized thousands, even though Israeli innovation and democracy makes the country the David of the Middle East, effective Palestinian and sympathetic European PR have no problem portraying Israel more as Goliath and the Palestinians as slingshot-wielding underdogs in this battle. This occurs even if groups like Hamas and Hezbollah have an inexhaustible supply of rockets with which to terrorize the civilian Davids and Davidas of Israeli cities and towns.

There remains a lively debate in the United States as to just how much the country should tie its foreign policy to Israel, especially in light of its burgeoning, rapidly growing Muslim population.

A book by American academics John Mearsheimer and Stephen Walt, called *The Israel Lobby and US Foreign Policy,* portrays groups like AIPAC (American Israel Public Affairs Committee) as "the tail that wags the American dog" on the matter of American foreign policy, and blames Zionist-leaning Jews in high places for America's fraught Middle East policy. The book underestimates the role played by America's endless appetite for Middle Eastern oil, and ignores similarities in the psychological mind-sets of right-wing American Jews and right-wing Christian evangelicals.

Increasingly, there are groups of Jews that speak out against the actions of Israel's right-of-centre governments, particularly regarding what they view as "collective punishment" of Palestinians, or successive Israeli governments' encouragement of illegal Jewish settlements in the West Bank. These organizations are small compared to mainstream American Jewish organizations, often founded by women, and have names like Jews for a Just Peace, Women in Solidarity with Palestine and Not In Our Name. Their voices harmonize with the large number of Israeli Jews who support Peace Now, a dissenting force in Israel that commands a good deal of respect within Israeli society.

Aside from Israel inadvertently providing flashpoints for anti-Semitism, there are occasional Jewish individuals who run amok and, as my mother would have it, "give Jews a bad name."

Shortly before I completed this essay, I heard of the exploits of one Bernard L. Madoff (aptly named, since he "made off" with so much of his clients' imaginary money). Madoff was a former president of NASDAQ. A one-man ethnic-reputation wrecking crew, he apparently used a Ponzi scheme to defraud investors, including many world-wide banks that should have known better, of some fifty billion dollars' worth of imaginary assets. Many of Madoff's victims were Jewish, including a large number of small Jewish charitable organizations, and large losses were incurred by banks in countries that historically either persecuted or even expelled Jews, like Austria, Spain, France, Switzerland and the United Kingdom.

Call it mildly paranoid, but Jews like me squirm whenever an alleged arch-villain has a first name like Bernard, Barney or Barrie (names which translate to the Hebrew *baruch* – meaning "blessed," the equivalent of the Swahili name Barack) and breathe a sigh of relief when the word "Junior" follows a villain's name, establishing him as probably *not* Jewish, since Jews almost never name their offspring after a still-living person. It shouldn't matter to me if a Bernie Madoff or another one-man wrecking crew, such as disgraced lobbyist Jack Abramoff, is Jewish ... but somehow it does. And I do worry, perhaps unnecessarily, about too much hay being made of it by those who make despising Jews a cornerstone of their identity. In tougher economic times, the hyperbolic views of such men are more likely to find more willing ears.

Jews are what I call the canaries in the mind-shaft; how they are treated predicts how other minorities, as well as women and gays, will eventually be treated. A large part of America's success story can be read in the motto of the Statue of Liberty and derives from just how thoroughly the country has embraced her minority groups.

In addressing an assembly of Christians United for Israel, the influential right-wing Pastor John Hagee said, "Those who bless Israel will be blessed and those who curse Israel will be cursed." While the neo-conservatives took this to mean blanket support for all of Israel's policies, the real meaning of the quote relates to how nations treat the Children of Israel as a people, as well as all their minority groups. Hagee added a line sure to make two-thirds of Jews (the liberal two-thirds) squirm: "Only the United States and Israel have been founded on religious faith."

The Ayatollah Khomeini would beg to differ.

Shame, Rage and Mideast Violence

Are people raised in fundamentalist societies more apt to hate others? (*The Toronto Star*, September 17, 2006)

Since the 1980s, Marvin Zonis, a political economist self-taught in psychology, has repeatedly warned there was more to the escalating violence in the Middle East than meets the eye. Challenging testimony given to a US Senate sub-relations committee, Zonis wrote, "Those committing violence against the US in Iraq have different ideological and political justifications for their actions ... But psychologically their justifications are driven by rage, the rage generated by deep narcissistic wounds. Narcissistic rage knows no boundaries and no limits."

We often ask, "Why do the Islamic fundamentalists hate us so much?" Zonis was asking a different question: "Why are they so good at hating?"

Are left-wing critics credible when they blame extremist violence on Western foreign policy, or on poverty? Or might something more elemental explain the shortage of good governance available to the fundamentalist Islamic nations of the Middle East? Could there be something in the fundamentalist upbringing of males that sets the stage for them, as adults, to blindly support charismatic types, be they dictators or holy men, who play on wounded pride and stir rage against a vilified other?

A recent essay by Thomas Homer-Dixon of the Trudeau Centre for Peace and Conflict Studies wisely advised against the folly of looking for a single factor to explain terrorism, and endorsed the need for more investigation into its multiple causes. "Participants in terrorism tend to be men in their twenties or thirties who are ferociously angry because of *powerful feelings of humiliation* (emphasis mine)." He identified a few potential sources of such humiliation, such as a lack of political and economic opportunity, then added that terrorists strongly identify with a group, society or culture they perceive as oppressed or exploited.

"Extremist leaders then inflame and manipulate these feelings of humiliation, partly by defining the 'enemy' – the group or society that's responsible for all problems and that should be the target of attack," Homer-Dixon said.

In this article I speculate about some psychological underpinnings that might lead young people to become "ferociously" angry and have "powerful" feelings of humiliation. But first a brief look at the differences between the emotions of shame and guilt is in order.

In classical psychoanalysis, shame is viewed as an earlier, more basic emotion than guilt, shame being tied to the very early phases in the formation of a cohesive sense of self.

By contrast, guilt feelings are developed later as the product of a more fully formed conscience, an achievement that only occurs once the child has given up intense libidinal and aggressive ties to early parenting figures.

Interference with normal development may cause a failure to neutralize these powerful bonds, a persistence of infantile narcissism and a later tendency to experience heightened shame and rage. Such interference may result from trauma with or without the early loss of parents, overindulgence or over-stimulation by parents or excessive use of punishment and other shaming techniques in child rearing.

If a child is repeatedly overwhelmed by shame and rage, he or she will have problems setting up abstract ideals and may, in order to shore up their sense of well-being as an adult, instead opt to serve idealized parent-like figures; they become those fervent men and women cheering at mass rallies in which hyperbole and blind allegiance are the norm.

Alternatively, a psychologically vulnerable person may create an idealized version of his or her own self in order to maintain internal balance. Such grandiosity typically requires a reviled other onto which one can project one's personal deficiencies – members of a rival sect, women, men, homosexuals or members of other races.

A psychoanalyst who extensively explored the origins of shame and rage in the human psyche was the late Heinz Kohut, founder of the school of therapy known as self psychology. His theories are useful in understanding and treating narcissistic personality disturbances. To Kohut, the development of a cohesive sense of self is a lifelong project, one that relies on a child receiving accurate empathy from his or her parents – a sense of being accurately "mirrored."

With their emphasis on suppressing the sexual drive and their elevation of the afterlife over life itself, many fundamentalist religions and sects are repressive in nature and resort to shaming people to keep them in line. They give strict directions at the expense of empathic understanding. They can provide their children with a coherent narrative but also with a groupthink that can lead to sanctioning the persecution of select groups that challenge that narrative.

Islamic fundamentalists are not alone in having a fraught psychology: Ohio State English professor emeritus Walter A. Davis recently wrote an interesting essay for *CounterPunch* in which he exposes the dangers of the literalism, the obsession with apocalypse and especially the troubled anti-sexual attitudes of the Christian fundamentalist right and how these have dovetailed with many of the blind spots of the Bush regime.

The shame/rage cycle is unpleasant to contemplate, but we ignore it at our peril. Even in the mass killings that traumatize our own society, we repeatedly hear that the young perpetrator "seemed depressed," "was a loner," "was abused by a parent" or "repeatedly taunted by his peers." We keep hearing that "he had a need to get even" with a particular group. How very rare are the exceptions to these rules.

Unfortunately, the shaming practices in fundamentalist societies are not widely discussed. In the case of the Muslim world, perhaps the only area where it is an active subject is in feminist discourse.

One of the more compelling, if strident, voices is that of Dr. Phyllis Chesler, a women's studies professor emeritus who wrote the books *Women and Madness* and, more recently, *The New Anti-Semitism.*

Chesler briefly lived in Kabul in the early 1960s as the wife of a Muslim man she had met in New York City. After only a few months of what she described as being "under house arrest in the tenth century," she fled back to the United States on her own. Chesler claims that widespread sexual abuses are common in Muslim, Afghan and Palestinian society.

In her article "The Psychoanalytic Roots of Islamic Terrorism," in which she paraphrases the work of Arabist Dr. Nancy Kobrin, Chelser writes:

> "The little girl lives her life under a communal death threat – the honour killing." Both male and female infants and children are brought up by mothers (who are debased and traumatized women). As such, all children are forever psychologically "contaminated" by the humiliated yet all-powerful mother. Arab and Muslim boys must disassociate themselves from her in spectacularly savage ways. But, on a deep unconscious level, they may also wish to remain merged with the source of contamination – a conflict that suicide bombers both act out and resolve when they manfully kill but also merge their blood eternally with that of their presumably most hated enemies, the Israeli Jews.

> In Kobrin's view, the Israeli Jews may actually function as substitutes or scapegoats for an even more primal, hated/loved enemy: Woman.

Chesler makes the inflammatory claim that, in the Muslim world, "widespread child sexual abuse leads to paranoid, highly traumatized and revenge-seeking adults." She also cites Kobrin's work describing "barbarous family and clan dynamics in which children, both girls and boys, are routinely orally and anally raped by male relatives; infant males are sometimes sadistically over-stimulated by being masturbated; boys between the ages of seven to twelve are publicly and traumatically circumcised; many girls are clitoridectomized; and women are seen as the source of all shame and dishonour and treated accordingly: very, very badly."

Chesler began her academic career as a leftist but turned right in response to what she came to see as the anti-Israeli and even anti-Semitic viewpoints increasingly prevalent on the far left of political discourse. As a Jew, a woman and a feminist, she has three sources of bias. As well, she often uses the word "Muslim" as opposed to "Islamic fundamentalist," thus aggravating the problem of an "us v. them" mentality. In the name of fairness, it needs to be pointed out here that, like fundamentalist Christians in the US, rigidly patriarchal Israeli Jewish families share some psychological features with their fundamentalist Muslim brethren.

In all three cases, males are overvalued relative to females. They are raised mainly by their mothers and then turned over to the tutelage and scrutiny of stern male teachers who are powerful father figures. If those teachers encourage in them a kind of compensatory narcissism, telling them that their religion or branch of their religion is the only true way, the results are predictable. It is an agonizing fact that the assassin of the late peacemaking prime minister Yitzhak Rabin came from a fundamentalist Jewish background. And James Charles Kopp, who in 1998 murdered an American doctor who practised abortion, was a devout Roman Catholic with links to fundamentalist sects.

However, Chesler is still right to question whether the child-rearing habits of Muslim fundamentalists contribute to an adult propensity for extreme violence. Few journalists seem willing to join the dots between the vilification of women, the mistreatment of children and the deeply pervasive sense of shame-and-rage reactions so readily exploited by Islamic leaders. To explore, let alone expose, such matters may provoke the very shame reactions that are so dangerously disproportionate. Journalists feel safer emphasizing less psychologically loaded, more proximal sources of humiliation, such as Israeli checkpoints and regular harassment by soldiers.

But they are missing the point. In his invaluable book *Shame and Pride,* Self Psychologist Donald Nathanson explains how the emotion of shame tends to be maximally generated when a person or group is physiologically geared up to have something very good happen, only to find the good feelings shattered by something bad happening instead.

It is the classical situation of being set up only to be disappointed. An example of this would be a parent who plans an elaborate family outing for his child, then cancels it at the last moment without explanation. For more global examples, consider what happens when the Iraqi people are expecting liberation from a dangerous dictator, only to find themselves, whether in the army or industry, thrown out of work by a transitional government hastily appointed and led by a blond, preppy American named Paul Bremer.

The "clash of civilizations" unfolding in the Middle East is thus, in part, a collision between an individualistic, guilt-based, Judeo-Christian tradition and a collectivist, honour-based Muslim culture that regards the shame of humiliation as the ultimate injustice. It is also a clash between religious fundamentalism and modernity, and religiously persecuted people everywhere, including women and gays, have a vital stake in it. (It is a bitter irony that the deposed Saddam regime was largely secular in nature, as are the governments of Syria, Lebanon and Israel.)

In short, men sensitized to shame by mistreatment at the hands of their parents and teachers are more likely to react with rage of psychotic proportions when they feel shamed in their adult lives. In the Middle East especially, there is no shortage of provocations around which to rationalize and justify extreme emotional responses.

The magnifying effects of the media ensure that every time an American or an Israeli bomb misses its mark, the resulting civilian deaths are piped into millions of Arab homes. Images such as those that came out of Abu Ghraib or the Hezbollah/Israel war waged on the backs of the Lebanese add exponentially to the collection of images likely to evoke shame and produce rage.

Does all this lead to suicide bombing? Narcissistic rage is a necessary – but not sufficient – contributor to that heinous act. Murder/suicides are, after all, highly orchestrated events and often involve coercion. Suffice to say that psychotherapists have long known the catastrophic results of the mixing of extreme religious views and suicide – as in the mass suicides of Jim Jones' People's Temple in Guyana and the cult religions of the Heaven's Gate and Solar Temple. To quote a remark by Sheik Hassan Nasrallah, the leader of Hezbollah, that is ominous for both Muslims and Jews, "The Jews love life, so that is what we shall take away from them. We are going to win, because they love life and we love death."

Psychotherapists also know that the first step in being able to manage powerful emotions is the ability to accurately identify them. A recent Hamas newspaper editorial gives us hope, then. Editor Ghazi Hamad, amid escalating violence in Gaza since Israel's withdrawal, called for Palestinians to examine their own behaviour rather than blaming Israel for all their problems. He stressed "self-criticism and self-evaluation," two character traits of which the entire Middle East is in urgent need.

In the meantime, both America and Israel would do well to avoid pushing the shame button as much as possible, and to avoid shaming responses to injured Muslim pride. And they should be aware that obstinate pride and a lack of self-awareness afflict both East and West. When I learned of the 1,776-foot-tall Freedom Tower soon to occupy the former World Trade Center site, my first thought was, "Where do they intend to paint the bull's eye?"

Afterword

Since I wrote this essay, there began to appear many whistle-blowing press articles meant to draw Western attention to the widespread discriminatory attitudes and practices prevalent in religious Islamic societies. One of the first books on the subjects was Azar Nafisi's best-selling *Reading Lolita in Teheran,* subtitled *A Memoir in Books,* about her experience teaching banned Western books to a clandestine group of female students. She followed up, in 2008, with a book titled *Things I've Been Silent About.*

In addition to making many observations of a deeply personal nature about her own parents, Nafisi reminds us that, while the age of marriage for women was eighteen in Iran, it was changed back to age nine after the Islamic revolution. Iranian women fought to have that delicate pre-pubescent age moved forward to thirteen, but sharia judges are still able to make exceptions for men who want essentially young girls as wives.

In an article in *The Globe and Mail* in 2008, called "Shame on Egypt's sexist bullies," award-winning journalist Mona Eltahawy, citing statistics compiled by the Egyptian Centre for Women's Rights, reported that two-thirds of two thousand Egyptian men surveyed admitted to harassing women. The majority blamed women for bringing on the harassment because of the way they dressed. More than 90% of foreign women visiting Egypt and more than 80% of native Egyptian women surveyed said they had been sexually harassed.

Eltahawy followed up in the *The Globe and Mail* with an article on spouse abuse called "The sister we missed," in which she makes it clear that, while spouse abuse is by no means confined to Muslim men, there are a disturbing number of sermons by "YouTube imams" that sanction the practice, preaching that there is no such thing as rape in marriage, and that husbands should learn to beat their wives without bruising them.

In his award-winning novel *The Yacoubian Building*, Alaa al Aswany describes a number of situations, largely influenced by poverty, in which women find themselves forced to tolerate sexual abuse by their employers or to submit to their lover's decisions on reproduction, as when one of his female characters, pregnant against her husband's stated will, is abducted, anaesthetized and forcibly aborted. Such abuses of power occur on a cultural as well as religious basis, and the fact that Muslim societies often deny the very existence of homosexuality, or advocate extreme punishments for it, make these sexual practices extremely dangerous and places those who engage in them at high risk for abuse and blackmail.

These accounts by female victims reached a crescendo pitch for me in an account by a Sudanese doctor, Halima Bashir, who was brutally beaten and gang-raped for having made public to the Western press some of the atrocities she witnessed. "Now you know what rape is, you black dog", excerpted in *The Globe and Mail* from the book *Tears of the Desert: A Memoir of Survival in Darfur*, is an excruciating piece of journalism as well as an account of great personal courage.

Another *Globe and Mail* article, by Saeed Shah, called "Tribal traditions and three girls' gruesome demise" gave an overview of the nearly seven hundred 'honour killings' reported to the authorities in Pakistan in the year it was published, and emphasized that a great many more such crimes go unreported.

Clearly in every culture there are instances in which men lord their greater physical power over women or, for that matter, over other men, but the degree to which extreme instances of the abuse of power are sanctioned either by culture or by religious edict relates particularly to this essay.

Writers such as Christopher Hitchens and the even more inflammatory Canadian author Mark Steyn (who, a small part of me wants to add, is not Jewish) repeatedly denounce "Islamo-fascism." Sometimes the tone of their writing further inflames the problem by overstating the extent to which such abuses are culturally or religiously sanctioned. It is more difficult, however, to deny those who have been victimized by such horrors, or only just narrowly escaped them, from making their case against religious or cultural sexism that, in the worst cases, reduces women to a sub-human status.

A fundamental problem with any essay on fundamentalism is that it makes it rather easy to equate the highly religious or orthodox with those who pursue fanatical re-education or even extirpation of those who do not share their views. Clearly, a man may fear that his fellows are at risk to burn in hell while adopting a tolerant view of their essential "right to be wrong."

Nor would I underestimate the dangers of Jewish fundamentalism. In October 2008, ultra-Orthodox Jews living in Acre, a city known for the peaceful co-existence of its Jewish and Arab citizens, stoned a car driven by an Arab man on the day of Yom Kippur. This soon resulted in rioting and the burning of several Arab and Jewish properties.

A joke once told to me by a female Orthodox patient voiced my misgivings about those who seek to *act* towards others on what I deem to be their pathological level of certainty:

> A man dies, goes to heaven and is offered a tour of the facilities by an angel. The first building the two pass by is a magnificent stone church. "How wondrous," exclaims the man, and the angel says, "Yes, this is where our Christians come to worship." Soon after, they approach a gigantic, ornate mosque. "Such splendid architecture," cries the man. "Yes, this is where our Muslims come to worship." The next building is a stately synagogue, finished in delicately carved wood and stone. "Let me guess," says the man, "This must be where Heaven's Jews come to worship." The angel nods with a smile. About a mile further down the path, the two arrive at a gigantic cardboard box with small air holes cut at the top. "My god, what is *this?*" exclaims the man. "Keep your voice down," whispers the angel. "This is where the fundamentalists worship, and they think they're the only ones here!"

Reflections on Jewish Identity

Were two, perhaps even three of Republican vice-presidential candidate Sarah Palin's grandparents of Jewish ancestry? Given that she was raised as a Christian, and is thought to have Mayflower ancestry, could this unsubstantiated rumour, that briefly caused a buzz on the Internet, about ethnic origins and "cultural DNA," possibly matter to anyone other than Jews and their perennial doppelgängers, anti-Semites? Sarah Palin was a tremendously polarizing figure. She was a ballsy female candidate who hunted moose. She said things about her opponent Barack Obama that could possibly have got him shot. I confess my heart jumped when I was sent an email with a link to this canard of a story about her 'real' Jewish roots.

It made me think: what is this multi-faceted thing called Jewish identity, especially in the context of a still peaceable North American diaspora? Jews breathe deep with pride when they learn that their co-religionists have been elected or appointed to positions of national power. Yet simultaneously, it may fill them with anxiety and dread.

On learning that President-elect Obama's first choice, White House Chief of Staff Rahm Emanuel, was Jewish, then hearing about two or three other Jewish picks, including Timothy F. Geithner, I confess to having the thought, "I hope he listens to much better Jews than President Bush did." Jews can, after all, walk among, and even lead both the cowboys and the bleeding hearts.

In the Fall of 2007, I had the honour of being invited to read at the annual Jewish Book Festival in Vancouver, and attended its opening gala, at which CBC radio host Eleanor Wachtel interviewed British author Howard Jacobson on his breakthrough book *Kalooki Nights*. The book is a *Bildungsroman* about growing up Jewish and working class in the city of Manchester, of a mother obsessed with the card game Kalooki and of her ineffectual husband, with whom the author, as a fictionalized youth, has a fraught relationship. In lieu of giving his son a bar mitzvah celebration at age thirteen, the father decides the boy needs to do something effective in the world. He therefore buys him a pair of boxing gloves. During one of the novel's most poignant scenes, father and son spar ineffectually in the courtyard while the boy's usually shy sister calls out, "Hit him, hit him!" unclear about who should hit whom.

Shy by temperament, and painfully aware of his own outsider status in British society, Jacobson nevertheless grew up seeing himself as more British than Jewish. He attended Cambridge University during the golden age of the literary critic F. R. Leavis, and came to share Leavis' preference for highly moral novelists such as Jane Austen and George Eliot, and for a while, his own writing sounded like those quintessentially English writers.

It was not until Jacobson started giving his central characters Jewish last names that he became aware of his own ethnic voice, but he also became painfully aware that few in British literary society were particularly interested in hearing that voice. He began to feel marginalized, a feeling intensified by the zeal with which British academics took up an anti-Israel stance and advocated unsavoury practices, such as boycotting Israeli scholars. In both the United Kingdom and France, the rapid growth in Muslim communities, largely unassimilated into mainstream British society, produced further anxieties among European Jews like Jacobson about a new kind of politically sanctioned anti-Semitism.

Unlike the hero of *Kalooki Nights,* Jacobson himself did have the requisite bar mitzvah. Nonetheless, he summarized his rather minimalist upbringing as a Jew as consisting of two directives from his father: first, Don't marry out and second, Stay *shtum,* meaning keep your mouth shut, especially about all matters Jewish.

Jacobson calls to our attention how few of the big-name writers in the United Kingdom have been Jewish, very unlike the situation in the United States. Jewish-by-birth British writers with assimilated last names such as Anita Brookner and Harold Pinter are scarcely recognizable as Jews. Jacobson suggested to Wachtel that the many pregnant silences in a Pinter play may have been all the Jewish bits left out, as Mr. Pinter himself remained *shtum* about a crucial aspect of his identity

These days one hears a lot about Jews choosing to leave, if not quite fleeing places like southern France and the United Kingdom, Argentina and Venezuela, out of fears of either Muslim anti-Semitism or politically motivated anti-Semitism on both the far right wing, which includes holocaust deniers, and increasingly commonly, the far left wing. The latter is particularly ironic, given that Jews, albeit assimilated or converted Jews like Karl Marx and Leon Trotsky, contributed to the very birth of the far left. Other Jews, such as Israel's most vocal American critic Noam Chomsky, are among the current left's most effective champions.

Despite Jacobson's candour, during the interview he never mentioned that he "looks" Jewish, or at least resembles the conventional stereotype of a Jew as a dark-haired, dark-eyed man with an olive cast to his skin and an ample Semitic (as in Jewish or Arabic) nose. A Jewish grandparent bequeathed France's remarkable president Nicolas Sarkozy the Semitic look, and something in the cultural DNA may have contributed to his choosing a Jewish foreign minister in Bernard Kouchner and, paradoxically, a ravishing female Muslim justice minister, Rashida Dati.

I do not mention the Semitic appearance issue to be vulgar. I mention it in recognition that Jacobson's experience of growing up Jewish in the United Kingdom would have been more that of a visible minority than mine was growing up in Canada. My own light brown hair and hazel eyes allowed me to "pass" for a typical third-generation Canadian (both my parents were indeed born in Winnipeg General Hospital, but ethnicity is ethnicity, especially in the eyes of one's enemies). I could blend in, especially when there might be anti-Semites around, while self-identifying as Jewish when it was to my advantage. Indeed, my parents felt, if not exactly proud, at least relieved that neither of their sons "looked Jewish." We were, after all, a minority group in fractious North End Winnipeg where Ukrainians, Poles, Germans and Jews either mimicked or begrudgingly admired one another, and it paid, most of the time, to try to fit in – again, in Jacobson's words, to stay *shtum.*

As with Jacobson's take on his dual British/Jewish identity, I regard myself as both Canadian and Jewish, though the latter might have been dominant were I born into an Orthodox family. Instead, my parents were not particularly observant as Jews, less observant of the Jewish holidays, in fact, than I have become. Their one abiding concern, aside from their boys knowing something about their Jewish heritage, was that we avoid intermarrying (Jacobson's "marrying out").

Unlike Jacobson and the thirteen-year-old boy he writes about, I did have a bar mitzvah, in Winnipeg's fabled North End in a slightly rundown Orthodox *schul* called The Ashkenazer, disparagingly nicknamed "the ash can" by secular Jews living in the neighbourhood. Standing proud, if a bit shaky on the elevated platform *(bimah),* I chanted my Torah portion to family, friends and a congregation of mostly elderly, mostly male believers (the women were up in the balcony) and I performed with sufficient verve to have received an ovation, were it a concert hall rather than a synagogue. Unlike most secularly raised Jewish boys schlepped by their parents to an Orthodox *schul* attended by their grandparents, my love of performance overcame my stage fright, along with any sense of not truly belonging and any concern that my passionate chanting might be somehow hypocritical.

The aging patriarchs who hold ultimate sway among the Orthodox of all religious faiths and ethnic creeds insist that their young charges place all else second to their religious and ethnic roots. They enforce clear rules about contact between males and females, as well as strict dietary practices, which reduces the opportunity of young people to fraternize with the youth of other religious groups or even with co-religionist peers who have more secular leanings, commonly referred to as "less observant" Jews. This encourages an "us versus them" mentality, and increases the cohesion of a small group that might otherwise be assimilated into the dominant society. There are Jews for whom the all too Christmassy colour combination of red and green is studiously avoided. The elders know that a drift away from tradition would leave them clinging to a world view that might be dismissed as antiquated. Such issues are writ even larger in Orthodox Islamic circles, as vividly portrayed in Alaa Al Aswany's novel *The Yacoubian Building*, an intriguing portrait of authoritarian, corrupt and class-ridden Egyptian society and a bestseller in the Arab world.

In Judaism, the branch called Modern Orthodox seeks to ensure that true believers cut themselves off less from the larger society. However, the more an Orthodoxy opens itself to the rest of society, the more prone it is to lose young people to intermarriage and the "ways of the stranger." Even among the Orthodox, about a third of the children marry out, though often they, or their families, press the non-Jewish partners to convert. In response, the Jewish Internet dating service 'JDate' now has a new category for users who are not Jewish, called "Willing to convert." (Matchmaking websites that cater exclusively to the *frum* have no use for such a category.) The usefulness of "Willing to convert" speaks not only to the desire of some Jews to look outside the religion for partners, but also to the desire of many gentiles to look to the mysteriously ancient tradition of Judaism as a way to centre their lives.

The shock of arrival of Jewish immigrants from the small towns (shtetls) of Eastern Europe in countries such as England and the United States was taken up in a long, difficult-to-read work called *Ordeal of Civility: Freud, Marx, Lévi-Strauss and the Jewish Struggle with Modernity.* Cuddihy's thesis is that Jews long used to an overcrowded, intimate and rough-hewn society of large, poor families arrived in a new world where people seemed not only unfriendly to them, but also distant and formal towards one another, and overly devoted to the rules of etiquette set out by the likes of Emily Post. Cuddihy suggests that the resulting painful sense of marginalization, coupled with this people's drive to formally educate their children, resulted in the brilliant, paradigm-challenging innovations of revolutionary Jewish thinkers.

Not that Cuddihy's thesis describes a situation unique to Jews. Irish immigrants also came from large, poor, agrarian families, as did Chinese immigrants of the early twentieth century. However, few would argue that the difficulty these groups had in "truly fitting in" often found expression in such issues as manners and formality, though such issues melted away by the third or fourth generation, as boardrooms and country clubs reluctantly opened their doors to the newcomers, at least those with shortened or anglicized last names. Whether Jewish thinkers like Freud, Lévi-Strauss or Marx were any more iconoclastic than non-Jewish émigrés absorbed into the Western establishment is highly debatable.

At a more personal level, the challenges Jewish families had adjusting to Western ways is taken up in the charming book *Unfinished People* by Ruth Gay, a touching and amusing evocation of the world of immigrant Jews in New York, where orthodox piety clashed with "American" newness. Chapter titles such as "Floors," "Chairs," "Awnings," "Hats," "Girls," "Beds" and "Corsets" speak to Gay's keen eye for the intimate details of trying to fit in with the ways of the new world.

If Eastern European Jews arrived in the New World without a taste for "high culture" outside their own religious culture, those who had become more established in Germanic countries tended to be less religious, and had something of a head start. The extent to which Jews are quick studies can be fully appreciated by strolling through the great museums of New York City, and reading the frequently Jewish names of the families who donated much of the art.

To take a less historic approach, and view things in terms of my personal history: I was once a baby on a table, and the Jews got to me first. During my nearly six decades on earth, an age similar to Jacobson's, I have come to feel as attached as he does to the Jewish people and their proud, if often harrowing heritage. However, I know this attachment is personal, and partly for aesthetic reasons. I love the poetry and ethical explorations of the sacred Jewish texts, the windmill-tilting, often dangerous quest to follow an ancient covenant and the aching beauty of their guttural tongues, Hebrew and Yiddish. The latter language is enjoying something of a revival, as befits a dialect that formed from a collision between the emotive Hebrew and the hyper-rational German. In the end, I am attached to many of Judaism's metaphors, though to the ultra-Orthodox, I and my wife and children are viewed either as barely Jewish or as Jews in need of religious rehabilitation.

An old friend with a Jewish and a Christian parent once stated that his ambition was to become "the hyphen in Judeo-Christian." That vow seemed much more radical at the time. Today, there is a biracial, arguably multi-ethnic president of the United States. The new Christian evangelicals have blurred the boundary line between Christianity and Judaism. They take up strongly pro-Israel positions, partly to facilitate the End of Days and what they view as the conditions needed for The Second Coming of the Messiah. (To the ever-patient, long-suffering Jews, the Messiah or *moshiach* has yet to make his appearance on earth. To Reform Jews, such issues are purely metaphoric.) I sometimes think that many evangelical Christians view themselves as the *real* Jews, taking Jesus as the divine reformer of Judaism, in the same way that Protestants might view themselves as the real Christians for having broken away from what was then a corruption-ridden, authoritarian Catholic Church.

After being converted to Christianity on the road to Damascus, St. Paul, formerly the Jewish Saul of Tarsus, was stricken blind, apparently so that he could see with more clarity. He decided that one could transform one's self from pagan to Christian through accepting Jesus alone, and, in the process, claim equal access to the promise given by God to Abraham and the chosen people, the Jews, a promise renewed through Jesus Christ. In other words, the road to salvation no longer need pass through the Jewish people and their complex body of laws and six hundred and thirteen blessed obligations or *mitzvot.* St. Paul even went so far as to call these laws a "curse," insofar as they were impossible for mere mortals to follow sufficiently. His denunciations of Jewish law set the stage for the gradual inversion of Jewish laws and Jewish ways by Christianity, such that the number thirteen became unlucky and headgear was removed, not put on, when entering a place of worship or a home. (Intriguingly, cardinals and the Holy Father himself still wear their headgear.)

St. Paul was, in the eyes of Orthodox Christians, the best kind of Jew, one who, like Sarah Palin, mistakenly labelled a Jewish convert centuries later, saw the light. Yet, if someone had attacked Sarah Palin as a Jewess who refused to colour within the lines drawn for her by the McCain campaign team, it would have set my teeth on edge.

Nothing fires up my sense of Jewish identity more than an encounter with anti-Semitism. It could be an anti-Semitic website, like Jew Watch or Real Jew News. A petition to remove the former from the Internet has been signed by hundreds of thousands of people. The latter of these two websites features slick, illustrated blogs by 'Brother' Nathanael Kapner, a Semitic-looking Jew who converted to Christianity, wears the garb of a monk and effectively promotes anti-Semitic sentiment. He regularly offers Joe McCarthy-esque lists of Jews who contribute to such diabolical causes as gun control. He portrays gun control as a Jewish plot to disarm gentiles and deprive them of their God-given right to self-defence. Though the majority of advocates for gun control have not been Jewish, it makes me proud to read the list of prominent Jews who have indeed advanced a cause dear to my own bleeding heart, from Congressman Emanuel Celler in 1968, to Senator Howard Metzenbaum and Member of Congress Dianne Feinstein, to Mayor Michael Bloomberg of New York and renowned lawyer Alan Dershowitz. Kapner missed mentioning that both liberal Jewish Justices of the Supreme Court voted against the right-wing-tilted, recent Court ruling on *District of Columbia v. Heller.* Nor does he seem to recognize that the first female president of the National Rifle Association (NRA), Sandy Froman, was raised in the San Francisco Bay area in a Jewish home. Facts like that would only set his argument back, and anti-Semites have very selective perceptions.

'Brother' Kapner also compiled an immensely long list of all the Jews ever associated with the Hollywood entertainment industry. I suppose the intention, here too, is to score points for a conspiracy, but no Jewish person can behold such a list without feeling proud and wondering if the industry could have ever achieved its worldwide pre-eminence without this star-studded cast of Jews – comparable to imagining the history of jazz without the contributions of African-Americans.

Needless to say, the bailout of Wall Street firms, some of which had Jewish names or Jewish CEOs, provides a potential windfall for anti-Semites. They delight in the demise or near-demise of firms with such Jewish names as Lehman Brothers or Goldman Sachs. The fallen insurance giant AIG's Jewish CEO Hank Greenberg gave them a golden opportunity to displace from collective memory the legendary Jewish baseball player with the same name. They will list the Jewish CEOs and avoid mention of the White Anglo-Saxon Protestants who dominate the financial field and the top Fortune 500 list of billionaires. They will point at George Soros, a man Jewish enough to have made Hitler's death list, even though he is private about his religious affiliations, while ignoring the Christian Bill Gates and Warren Buffet, non-Jews with more than ten times the wealth of Mr. Soros. To remain consistent in its paranoid hatred, Jew Watch lists both Mr. Buffet and Mr. Gates as Maranos, (Sephardic Jews from Spain and Portugal forced to convert to Catholicism but who secretly remained Jewish).

One might think that anti-Semites who invoke a world banking conspiracy might have thought to include the Swiss, known for their impenetrable and far more extensive banking practices than, say, the Rothschild family, but again, Jew-haters are wonderfully selective in their judgment.

I suppose that, if Jews can play the name-game, proudly listing those among their small numbers who have challenged conventional wisdom, so can anti-Semites, albeit with a totally different emphasis.

Two successive Jewish Chairmen of the Fed named Greenspan and Bernanke served the class interests of Christian power-brokers like Bush, Cheney and Rumsfeld, only to be replaced by another, more liberal-minded, and far more WASP-ily named Obama appointee, Timothy F. Geithner, to whom Wall Street looks as the next potential saviour. Liberal Jews like me hope that Geithner will acquit himself better in his post than did Alan Greenspan, though many people made a handsome living while Greenspan was at the controls, hanging on his every word for hints as to whether to buy, hold or sell. Of course, these men's cultural or religious affiliations would be of little or no interest in a world free of anti-Semites, or for that matter, chauvinistic or partisan Jews, any more than we should care that the likes of Henry Paulson Jr. are *not* Jewish.

Jew-baiting websites like Real Jew News and Jew Watch may have sprung up as a reaction to pro-Jewish, largely conservative sites like Jewish World News, which features both Jewish columnists as well as philo-Semitic, strongly pro-Israel gentile columnists like George Will and Ann Coulter (whom anti-Semites deride as "Jew lovers").

Recently, business scion Edgar Bronfman Sr., interviewed in *The New York Times,* stated that he considers anti-Semitism spent as a world force. To him, a clear sign of its weakening was when Joe Lieberman ran for vice-president of the United States and there did not appear to be much of a backlash around his religion. He also believes that a landmark change in Judaism's fate occurred once Jews withdrew their longstanding reluctance to accept converts.

I am less inclined to share Mr. Bronfman's sanguine conclusion, though perhaps a downturn in anti-Semitic feeling in North America had as much to do with the long-running TV series *Seinfeld* and the ubiquity of the Jewish bagel as anything else. Barbara Streisand too kept her Semitic nose and sounded all the right notes for her people. Nor did it hurt that powerful Australian media baron Rupert Murdoch, who runs, among other media outlets, FOX News, is a philo-Semite who loves and promotes Israel and her many achievements in science and technology.

However, whenever there is a steep economic downturn, Jewish people know that populist movements can spring up led by men who finger The Jews as the cause for whatever has gone wrong. This happened during the worldwide market crash of the 1840s, when a Jewish conspiracy was blamed for cheap American commodities flooding the markets and wiping out competition in Europe. Among the people who lost everything was the father of Sigmund Freud. No wonder Freud once remarked, "America is a mistake; a gigantic mistake, it is true, but nonetheless a mistake."

To my mother's credit, unlike Howard Jacobson's father, she never advised me to stay *shtum.* Instead, she warned that the worst anti-Semites are Jewish anti-Semites. She said this without ever having read a single word by American authors Noam Chomsky or Norman Finkelstein (whose latest paper was titled "In Defense of Hezbollah") or by Canadian author Naomi Klein, who are far more rational than 'Brother' Kapner in their sharp criticism of Israel. Their words are vexing to all but more left-leaning Jews. These secular Jewish authors, whom conservatives would dismiss as bleeding hearts, are also fiercely critical of American foreign policy, which they see Israel as a mere extension of, and the often acidic tone of their writing counterpoints that of more right-leaning lawyer Alan Dershowitz, author of the books *Chutzpah* and *The Case for Israel.* Some would dismiss him, or other right-wing Jews like Irving and William Kristol, Paul Wolfowitz, Daniel Pipes, David Frum and Charles Krauthammer, as cowboys for their enthusiastic defence of the invasive foreign policy of the Bush administration.

Anti-Semites exist even in countries with few or no Jews. As long as they do, many Jews, religious or secular, will be vocal about our people's many virtues. At the same time, many may choose to remain *shtum* about our faults, or limit such discussion to their own group, in the spirit of the old, defensive Yiddish phrase, *A shande far de goyim* (a disgrace before the gentiles). The phrase was used by Yippie activists Abbie Hoffman and Gerry Rubin as they taunted their fellow-Jew, Judge Julius Hoffman at the Chicago Seven trial, after he ordered that protestor Bobby Seale, who refused to stay *shtum* in the courtroom, be bound and gagged.

If it is not unusual to find Jews at both the far left and the far right of many social causes, it's because each of my co-religionists has his or her own take on *Tikkun Olam* and we are not shy. *Chutzpah* is one of our core secular values, especially in these modern times when violent oppression of Jews has given way to the tolerance that follows cultural pluralism. Many of us are willing to go public with our views, even when they include unflattering opinions on Judaism and all things Jewish, even if it causes our brethren some anxiety. Of course, Jews of my or Howard Jacobson's vintage never experienced the same degree of oppression as did Jews of my father's vintage, and he in turn, with his Winnipeg birth, did not see anything like what his father did on the fearsome steppes of the Ukraine.

Perhaps the impressive rise of Jewish influence is about to be displaced by the meteorically rising influence of diasporic South Asians or Chinese. Who, after all, has more *chutzpah* than the Semitic-looking Salman Rushdie? He spoke metaphoric truth to fundamentalist power, and had to go into hiding for years to escape the death edict of a *fatwa.*

Like Howard Jacobson, I am reluctant to add my own confessional offerings to the enormous mountain of dirty laundry. Nonetheless, I would like to take these reflections in a more personal direction and return to the issue of visible minority status as it related to Jewish identity.

I was once a member of a Reform Jewish friendship circle, or *chavura,* at the Holy Blossom Temple. One evening, as the group of a dozen men and women were sitting around in my living room, trying to think up new ideas for evening programs, I made what struck others as a very amusing suggestion: "Why don't we each wear a *yarmulka* (skullcap) for a week, and then get together and discuss how we felt about doing it?"

Needless to say, the idea was greeted as more of a jest than a serious proposal. One does not easily give up the invisibility of being relatively assimilated for wearing any kind of sign saying "I am a Jew." This, despite the fact that even quite secular Jews are willing to adorn their door posts with decorative *mezuzahs* that identify which houses are the homes of Jews.

Let me offer another example.

In the Departures lounge of Toronto's Pearson airport, on American Thanksgiving Day, my wife and I and some friends from our temple, while awaiting our plane's arrival, beheld a uniquely Jewish spectacle. A heavy-set man, in black Orthodox garb and a full grey beard, who weighed as much as Howard Jacobson and myself combined, decided to perform in a public place the religious ritual of putting on phylacteries or *tefillin.* This is an elaborate ritual obligatory for Orthodox Jews, one that involved this gentleman carefully winding long, leather straps around his powerful arms, donning a tiny square leather hat that contains a prayer and then draping his entire person inside an enormous prayer shawl or *tallit.* He worked away without apparent self-consciousness, and with some relish. He stood very close to where other passengers were seated, having decided there was no need to step away from the crowds to a somewhat more discreet location in the nearly deserted airport waiting area. He seemed oblivious to how others who were unfamiliar with such a religious ritual might react to its foreignness. Not for him, the old warning, *Shande far de goyim.*

Like others in the waiting area, I found myself drawn to secretly observing his technique. After all, the putting on of *tefillin* is, in Judaic law, an obligatory act performed on a daily basis. Indeed, I have been accosted on the street by Orthodox Jewish youth who have offered to teach me how to put on *tefillin,* after they flagged me down with the rather arresting, overly familiar question, "Are you Jewish?"

Was this man being merely relaxed, was he oblivious or something of an exhibitionist? I subsequently ran the question by a number of Jewish people who share with me the liberal-reform level of religious observance. On a day-to-day basis, we Reform Jews decide not to perform a variety of religious rituals prescribed by the Torah, though we try to inform our daily conduct with Jewish principles of decency and good will to others. Our religious performance is limited to consecrating the Sabbath and to attending holiday gatherings at which our rabbis, in a sense, lead us in performing rituals and sometimes perform them on our behalf, in the spirit of the temple priests of the past.

The religious display by one praying man wrapped in his prayer shawl took place in Pearson International's ultra-modern Terminal One. At the same time, the oversized, high-definition television screens were filled with gruesome news about terrorist attacks on the citizens of Mumbai, which claimed dozens of lives and injured hundreds. Among those murdered by youthful gunmen were a rabbi, his wife and others who worked at or attended an Orthodox *Chabad* centre. It might seem preachy on my part to expect a fellow Jew more religiously 'observant' than myself to recognize that the TV screen in the waiting area was broadcasting the devastating effects of Islamic fundamentalism; that those, like me, who were waiting for their plane, might be uneasy about witnessing any kind of ultra-religious ceremony being performed by someone about to join us on a plane trip to New York City. The thought "Why here? Why not do that a bit further down the departures area?" was clearly a screen for a deeper thought, such as, "Get out of my face with your religiosity!" Was I, like comedian Bill Maher, who conceived of the movie *Religulous,* someone who Rabbi David Wolpe might argue was "viscerally" offended by the sight of Orthodox religious display?

"Sometimes," said that self-declared Godless Jew Sigmund Freud, "a cigar is just a cigar." This impressive, male-centred religious performance was only such for those who, like me, would serve as a rapt, if also slightly resentful audience. By so publicly putting on his *tefillin,* this man was making himself even more uniquely visible as a member of a minority group, as it happens, my minority group, smack dab in the middle of the departures area of a Toronto *international* airport.

What I had observed may have been globalism at its best, even as the TV screens told of a different story, the psychotically vicious, counter-reaction to globalism by fundamentalists whom I would bet had only a brief, if intense, indoctrination in a fanatical strain of Islam. His public religious act was a source of shame for me, initially, then reactive resentment, and I hope to understand how I and the rest of humanity can learn to better deal with our need for aggressive wishes towards our fellow men that occasionally boil to the surface.

Intolerance by the ultra-Orthodox cost Israel its great, peacemaking president, the assassinated Yitzhak Rabin. It also resulted in the machine-gun massacre, by Baruch Goldstein, of Muslim men kneeling at prayer, this, of course, being a psychotically rage-filled response to equally horrible atrocities committed by the other side. Was I also showing my own, if oh-so-liberal version of intolerance by unleashing this multitude of reflections about the performance of a single, if drawn-out act of piety in a public, somehow un-Jewish place?

Jews are the canaries in the "mind-shaft." The good fortune of countries who treat Jews well rises, and the fortune of those who persecute or even exterminate them falls, not only because they lose out on what the Jewish tradition has to offer, but because they inevitably persecute all minorities within their borders, which leads to internecine conflict, and to intervention by the more enlightened world.

This Yom Kippur, on the Day of Atonement, I will ask forgiveness of the large patriarchal man who so successfully caught and held my attention with his unabashed, or should that be unapologetically, open religious display. The psychiatrist in me will speculate about the role played by my unresolved 'Oedipal issues' in determining the strength of my response.

Borat's Inner Jew

The unsaid truth about Sacha Baron Cohen's clownish alter ego.
(*The Toronto Star,* November 12, 2006)

On the most obvious level, the film *Borat* is the perfect vehicle for British (and modern Orthodox Jewish) prankster, actor and TV star Sacha Baron Cohen. It is an over-the-top tale of the haplessly male-chauvinist, sex-obsessed, strangely lovable Kazakh character Borat Sagdiyev, a naive foreigner who journeys through America in search of its redemptive surface glamour, as embodied by Pamela Anderson and the universally welcoming evangelism of the southern Christian right.

But beyond Baron Cohen's outlandish shtick, *Borat* has several timely ingredients that ensure its relevance. In an era when any olive-skinned, moustachioed man travelling without his family just might get mistaken for a terrorist, the issue of basic trust is a big one. This is a movie about the post-9/11 United States, immigration, anti-Semitism and xenophobia.

And on a deeper, even subconscious, level, it's about the wandering, out-of-place Jew, and the fear and hysteria he causes based on classic anti-Semitic stereotypes.

Borat is the lovable naïf who is unaware or unconcerned about how others might react to his racism and misogyny. He offers commentary on such alleged Kazakh festivals as "the running of the Jew" without batting his long, curly eyelashes.

But even while playing his outrageous alter ego, Baron Cohen remains a Jew. This dual identity provides the viewer with welcome relief, because he is harmless as a foreigner, as a Jew and as a Muslim.

Borat-as-Muslim, along with his overweight producer-friend Azamat, brings along a live chicken, but neither seems to have access to a weapon, let alone a bomb belt.

Moreover, this Jewish actor is more than willing to undergo all manner of personal degradation in the quest to be loved by modern America. Borat-as-Jew knows his place and finally settles into a loving relationship with a member of another frequently disparaged minority group, an African-American prostitute.

Borat-as-immigrant, meanwhile, also has the good sense to return to Kazakhstan rather than take a job away from an American.

But a close examination of Borat reveals something else – that the Orthodox Baron Cohen has given this clownish anti-Semite all the stereotypical traits of the secular Jew, a type characterized by a dyed-in-the-wool individualism that has flowered several times in modern history, each time challenging both the God-centred and man-centred view of the universe in ways that would have been understood by Copernicus, Galileo and Darwin.

First came Moses, who led a slave revolt of one particular people against the reigning power of the day, the empire of Egypt. Moses championed the Abrahamic stance against the idolatry and multiple gods but also transformed the Jews into a fighting force capable of retaking the Holy Land from the various tribes that occupied it.

The next Jewish-born (albeit non-practising) force to re-centre the world was Karl Marx, whose socialist doctrine threatened such core conceptions as the growth of capital in the hands of select elites and the right to personal property.

A third great Jewish-born thinker, Sigmund Freud, told humanity that the mind is largely influenced by unconscious forces and not by the higher powers of human reason. Among the concepts Freud pioneered that were particularly unsettling were those of infantile sexuality, an Oedipus complex that involved attractions to both parents and a universal unconscious mind teeming with both intensely sexual and aggressive fantasies.

A fourth secular Jewish thinker, Einstein, set the world of science spinning by debunking many of the Newtonian certainties that had come to be accepted as gospel. He posited the concept of a "relativity" that was every bit as disorienting as Moses's exclusive monotheism, Marx's fetish about the primacy of the worker as sole source of the means of production, and Freud's emphasis on unconscious forces against which human reason must do endless battle if the human species is not to destroy itself through pointless war.

Even today, consider the effective outsider send-up of American culture delivered by comedian Jon Stewart of *The Daily Show.* Stewart shows film clips from American political life that look as absurd as the 'documentary' footage taken by Borat and Azamat. When challenged on

Howard Stern's show about his *real* name, Jon Stuart Liebowitz, Stewart answered, "Actually, it's Jewy Jewman."

Which brings us to one of the core, subconscious aspects of the film: the self-assured, sexually decadent and breast-obsessed Borat satires many of the stereotypes about Jews held by Christians ever since St. Paul turned the core of Christianity into a religion wary and critical of all but the most wedlocked sexual activity.

The Jews as a people were exiled from the Holy Land and condemned to wander the earth as a powerless minority at the whim of the hostile urges of Christian and Muslim hosts. Until the Enlightenment of the eighteenth century, most Jews looked and dressed differently from people in the countries that allowed them refuge and were always at the mercy of popular myths that cast them as dirty and depraved, or alternatively, as all-powerful and harbouring designs to take over the world.

In "The Protocols of the Elders of Zion," a fraudulent document believed to have been produced by the Russian secret police, Jews were portrayed as intending to overthrow Christianity through subversion and sabotage, and to control the world. This treacherous portrait of a tiny religion that has never numbered more than thirteen million souls is often evoked by anti-Semites, many of whom still reside in the very Russia from which hundreds of thousands of Jews have fled to Israel over the past fifty years.

In *Borat,* it is a hospitable, elderly Jewish couple that wouldn't hurt a fly that makes Borat and Azamat cower in terror. But it is myths about the power of Jews (and Gypsies) and claims such as "The Protocols" that add to the vehemence of the anti-Semitism in the countries that once made up the Soviet Union. That many of the countries ending in "stan" are mainly Muslim can only complicate their world view of Jews, given the long-standing conflict between the Muslim Arab world and Israel.

These speculations about ethnicity might seem like far too much to read into a dumb prankster flick that has people snorting with glee into their turtlenecks. But all comedy revolves around deeply, if often unconsciously, experienced truths, and indeed, the reversal of such truths. To lampoon Kazakhs as virulent anti-Semites even while portraying a Kazakh in a manner congruent with classic caricatures of a Jew – now that's *chutzpah!*

The Chutzpah of Atheists

On Yom Kippur, 2007, I attended a study session that Toronto's Holy Blossom Temple offers its congregants during their uncomfortable fast. The session was moderated by engaging CBC news anchor Evan Solomon, who provocatively titled it, "The Case against God." Solomon reviewed with his audience the criticisms of religion/religiosity advanced in recent books by what he jokingly referred to as "militant atheists." These include Sam Harris's *The End of Faith,* scientist Richard Dawkins' best-selling *The God Delusion* and journalist Christopher Hitchens' book with the still more prickly title, *God Is Not Great,* and downright inflammatory subtitle, *How Religion Poisons Everything.*

Before going into journalism, Solomon majored in religious studies. He is not shy about the fact that, while a believer from an early age, he went into religious studies because of lingering doubts about the existence and true nature of God.

Aware that most of his audience were familiar with the *Jewish* case for God, Solomon briefly reviewed Christian thinkers such as Thomas Aquinas, Anselm and French philosopher/mathematician Blaise Pascal, whose famous "wager" posited that since we cannot prove whether or not God exists, we may as well *possibly* be on the winning side of the debate. Solomon pointed out that, as a religion, Judaism concerns itself more with the human effort to perfect this world *(Tikkun Olam)* than about rarified ontological and teleological debates, though those are taken up at great length in some rabbinic commentaries on the Torah.

Solomon spoke to how simple-minded conceptions of God, i.e. God as a man with a white beard in the sky who knows everything and can do everything, are easily attacked by the likes of Dawkins and Hitchens. He shared with the audience the two men's undisguised contempt for issues of "dependency" that propel people into believing in an essentially benevolent deity, despite a wealth of disturbing evidence against the existence of a just and caring God. Believers have a tendency to hand-pick certain principles from their sacred texts while blithely choosing to ignore others that cast the Divine One in a less flattering light. Solomon repeated Dawkins' assertion that, while there are devastating religious wars, no wars have been carried out in defense of atheism. This made me think of the anti-clerical purges of the Mexican Revolution and the anti-Russian-Orthodox purges that were part of the Russian Revolution. Chairman Mao, anyone?

Solomon had himself once interviewed Dawkins, and asked the man if science can explain the deep feelings of love that he, Evan Solomon, feels towards his children. While serotonin and dopamine surges might be involved, as well as evolutionarily selected principles of self-preservation, could that *really* explain parental love any more than analyzing the brushstrokes of a Van Gogh or the notes of a Beethoven symphony can capture the essence of the painting or symphony? To which scientist Dawkins responded with, "Give us time ..."

At one point Solomon asked this audience of fasting Jews, who were as thirsty for water as for knowledge, for a show of hands by those who believed in God, then another by those who claimed to be atheists. Only one valiant hand rose for the latter. He then asked how many found the question too complicated to answer in a Yes or No fashion, Predictably, up went the hands of about two-thirds, many of whom were well-heeled professionals.

During the question period that followed the talk, esteemed senior rabbi from Hamilton, Bernard Baskin, declared that, recently, he had been called upon to comfort a dying woman, who pleaded, "Am I in God's hands?" The rabbi had known exactly what to say, and wondered how Mr. Dawkins or Mr. Hitchens would have replied to a human being so desperately in need of consolation. But then, neither Dawkins nor Hitchens opted to go into the helping or healing professions.

I would have liked to have stood up and offered a few words, but my throat was bone-dry, my breath foul from the fast and my heart beat away at the thought of rising and saying something that might prove less than memorable.

I might have offered that the real problem in today's world is not religion, but religious fundamentalism. Or, in the words of a Yom Kippur sermon by another senior rabbi at Holy Blossom, Edward Goldfarb, "The Torah is meant to be treated, not literally, but *literarily.* Its ideas must be allowed to evolve in the modern world much as scientific ideas have had to evolve over time. We don't throw out scientific thinking, for example, just because many of Newton's ideas are now dated."

Alas, those would have been knee-jerk reactions on my part.

Looking back, here is what I *really* would have liked to have said: "Personally, I am agnostic intellectually, but a believer emotionally." It is a qualified stance reminiscent of Pascal's "The heart has reasons the mind cannot understand." Who *is* Mr. Hitchens to dismiss religion as an unhealthy "dependency" when he himself seems to struggle with dependence on cigarettes and alcohol? But that is just "the hot-thought," the *ad hominem* portion of my response.

Cooling down, I would suggest that atheism, the claim that God does not exist, makes less sense when compared to, say, agnosticism, especially if one accepts what science has revealed to us about the awe-inspiring dimensions of the known universe. The claim smacks of intellectual over-reaching, even *chutzpah*. Allow me this metaphor: consider two talking aphids debating whether there is anything more all-powerful than a carpenter ant, the latter being an irresistible force that can take them into bondage or release them at will and administer punishment of divine proportion. Along comes a third aphid, who says, Ah, but I know that there is a winged god far mightier than the carpenter ant, for I have seen its huge presence swoop down and carry off several carpenter ants in its mighty beak. Clearly that winged presence must be the one *true* God!

To Hitchens' credit, he eschews the label atheist, and prefers to label himself an "anti-theist," a man who is simply certain that none of the arguments in favour of God can stand the light of close scrutiny.

From a cold scientific perspective on this vast universe, human beings are as aphids, albeit highly intelligent ones. We ought to be suspect of the reach of our pet theories on the absolute meaning of things. Most of us start out as babies on a table, and the followers of one particular religion that get to us first sell us on compelling myths and metaphors and poetic vision of humanity, not to mention music, costumes and ceremonial food. Religion, then, partly depends on aesthetic as well as a moral choice. Being aware of that ought to make one very reluctant to foist their own religion on others. One should rather take the attitude of the Orthodox rabbi towards the would-be convert, and feel obliged to refuse the convert's request three times before welcoming him or her into the fold.

Religion also helps us shrink an impossibly large world down to manageable proportions. Without congregations, religions would be greatly impoverished. "Why do you come to synagogue?" Hymie asks Yankel, in an old joke, who responds, "Rosenberg says he comes here to talk with God." "Never mind Rosenberg, why do *you* come to *schul?"* Yankel scratches his head, then answers, sheepishly, "I come to talk with Rosenberg."

Following the study session, the audience repaired to religious services endowed with the beauty of Hebrew liturgy, an ancient music enriched with minor chords that play the heart like a fiddle, eloquent sermons and both young and old congregants performing feats of cantillation.

Will Dawkins and Hitchens one day come to understand that the ineffable beauty of such services cannot be dismissed as mere subservience? Perhaps these determined scientists experience such beauty in well-founded scientific argument, and in scientific colloquia that provide them with the equivalent of congregation. If so, I wish them each a *mazal tov* and a healthy and happy year to come, with or without God's help.

When I asked a close friend of mine who is a psychiatrist if he believed in god, he answered that God's existence is quite independent of his own pet theories. We agreed that some people's brains are more wired to be believers than others' and just left it at that. Neither of us was keen on placing the matter of our belief in a divinity, which waxed and waned, at the core of how we viewed ourselves.

To those who extol rationality, God *may* be little more than "Good Odds." My father-in-law, Martin J. Cohen, a physicist who invented the ion mobility spectrometer that tests for explosives at airports, thinks of God that way, and once, he referred to cathedrals and temples as "God boxes." Legally blind yet still vibrant at eighty-seven, he is living proof that there are indeed atheists in foxholes, if one may consider old age a foxhole. I would embrace his purely rational formulation, if it did not leave me cold.

Atheists aren't the only ones with *chutzpah.* American celebrity Pastor Joel Osteen of the Lakewood Church and Joel Osteen Ministries, sings the praise of a personal God who takes time out to care that each worthy person get a good parking spot every day! His Pollyanna portrait of a feel-good, micromanaging God leaves me exasperated.

Since I wrote this, a new book has come out, called *The Devil's Delusion,* subtitled *Atheism and its Scientific Pretensions,* by David Berlinski, who seeks to put Dawkins, Hitchens and Harris in their place, and attributes many of the worst excesses of the violent twentieth century to its prevailing lack of faith. What the century lacked in faith, however, it made up for in its zealotry for utopian, totalitarian reshaping of the world, whether in the name of communism, Nazism or the Cultural Revolution.

An effective Canadian film that was made to denounce capitalism, called *The Corporation,* forgot to mention that one of the good things about corporations is that they *make things.* Similarly, by trashing religions as being nothing more than ways of perpetuating worn out, unlikely tales about creation and the origins of good and evil, atheists fail to appreciate the role religious education plays in insisting that young people look at ethical issues, rather than sink into complacency.

Humanists like Canadian oncologist Dr. Robert Buckman, author of *Can We Be Good Without God?,* would point to alternatives to religious education for awakening an awareness of moral issues in young people, but an equally compelling moral infrastructure is, at least for now, simply not available.

The presumption of certainty on either side of this never-ending debate obliges me to don the scarlet letter of agnosticism, even as I restate my own inner need for meaning laced with mystery, as opposed to ultimate scientific rationalization. Perhaps it is a matter of having a number of shifting selves, at least one of which is a believer.

This unscratchable itch was captured by Danish poet Piet Hien in his poem "I'd like –" from his bestselling poetry book, *Grooks,* which I read as a boy:

> I'd like to know
> What this whole show
> Is all about
> Before it's out.

Acknowledgements

In the late sixteenth century, Michel de Montaigne of Bordeaux initiated a sustained exercise in self-reflection, a book he titled *Essais,* which literally means attempts, trials or soundings. When Wolsak and Wynn publisher Noelle Allen asked for a collection of essays, I was uneasy about my own attempts, and aware that my North-End-Winnipeg-Jewish roots might show. However, Montaigne reassures: "Every man bears the whole stamp of the human condition."

A writer is a consortium that forges links between the best viewpoints and the best opinion and evidence to which he is exposed, in my case, by other authors, but also by friends, colleagues, rabbis, clients (in my case, they go under the misnomer "patients") and, of course, family members. I first ran my prose by a professional editor, Susan Ioannou, who helped me polish and tighten. As I began to get essays and articles accepted more frequently by Canadian newspapers, I received editing by a number of publications, including *The Medical Post,* where, for sixteen years, I was contributing poetry editor.

None of the above prepared me for the to-and-fro, pitched email battles with the former Ideas editor of *The Toronto Star,* Peter Scowen, who has now moved to *The Globe and Mail.* So much of my unsolicited material ended up on Peter's cutting-room floor that I despaired of having anything left to say, but gradually, by accretion and a host of eleventh-hour afterthoughts and corrections made possible by our mutual forbearance, an essay would emerge, often different from the one I had intended to write, but generally, more readable and with fewer punches pulled.

The following essays first appeared in *The Toronto Star:* "Shame, rage and Mideast violence," "Guns, Lethality and the Big Lie," "Love, Death and Old Men," "Don't Call me White" and "Borat's inner Jew." The essays "Death at arm's length" and "Can Lassie afford to get medical help?" first appeared in *The Medical Post.* Selected letters first appeared in *The Toronto Star, The Globe and Mail, The National Post* and *The Seattle Times.*

The essay "A Poet and a Psychiatrist" is reprinted with permission from the Literature, Arts and Medicine blog of New York University (http://medhum.med.nyu/blog). The book review of *Poets on Prozac* is reprinted with the permission of *The American Journal of Psychiatry.*

These essays were enriched by the opinions of bright and highly articulate friends who have accompanied me and my dog Buttons on long walks through neighbourhood ravines or who have matched wits with me in fireside chats. They sometimes agree, sometimes disagree, with my views and have been my first, though by no means last, critics. They include, in alphabetical order, David Baskin, Elliott Bronstein, Roo Borson, Alice Charach, Jon Ennis, Joan Garson, Sophie Glazer, Laurence Gottleib, Jay Harris, Len Leven, Jack Micay, Andy Patton, Louis Peltz, Rivanne Sandler and Klaus Willmann. Jon Ennis drew my attention in a very timely way to key articles on guns in the medical literature.

The conversation with a female poet friend in "So, why do you write?" was recalled more than a week after it occurred, and was no doubt altered in the process of remembering.

Knowing I am a writer, colleagues in psychiatry often refer me highly articulate men and women, some of whom are knowledgeable in areas like politics, popular culture, pornography and video games. They set me straight whenever we exchange views. Rules of confidentiality make it wrong to name them, but they know of my debt to their willingness to share their views and to occasionally steer me to just the right book or website.

Thanks, for the second time, to John Brown and the Olga Korper Gallery for their willingness to share yet another of John's wonderfully crafted paintings, and to Ken Priestley, who did the cover design.

Noelle Allen asked for these essays, and shaped the manuscript from the reams of material I sent her. She then had the patience and interpersonal skill to help me deliver on her request, and she and Ashley Hisson held my feet to the fire with fact checks. Lindsay Hodder provided diligent editorial assistance.

Noelle believed that a poet – and practicing psychiatrist – should have the opportunity to make a statement in the medium of "creative non-fiction" prose.

Notes

Arms and the Man

1. James Gilligan, *Violence: Reflections on a National Epidemic* (New York: Random House, 1997).
2. Richard Feldman, *Ricochet: Confessions of a Gun Lobbyist,* (New Jersey: John Wiley & Sons, 2006).
3. Rodrigo Bascunan and Christian Pearce, *Enter the Babylon System: Unpacking gun culture from Samuel Colt to 50 Cent* (Toronto: Random House, 2007).
4. Terrence Real, *I Don't Want to Talk about It: Overcoming the Secret Legacy of Male Depression* (New York: Simon & Schsuter, 1998).

The Trouble with Tasers

5. Ron Charach, "The Real Danger with TASERs," *National Post,* September 19, 2008.
6. Editorial, "When to Zap," *National Post,* September 15, 2008.
7. T. J. Kaye, "Safe Zapping," *National Post,* September 19, 2008.
8. Aaron Aupperlee, "Real or Fake: Law enforcement officers concerned about blurring between deadly and toy guns," Desert Dispatch, February 14, 2008, http://www.desertdispatch.com/onset?db=desertdispatch&id=2589&template=article.html.
9. Brahim Resnik, "Jim's Gun Supply Paints Guns to Look like Toys," *CNN News,* February 19, 2008.
10. Frederic Zalac, "The Taser Test," *CBC News,* December 5, 2008.

Since this essay was written, a spate of articles emerged on the use of tasers on minors, whether in custody or as a means of coercing greater compliance with the police. A lively, long overdue debate is now taking place on both sides of the border as to the ethics of such uses of the device, and Wikipedia is publishing the names of all those who die after having received taser shocks.

Guns, Lethality and the Big Lie

11. Demetri Sevastopulo, "US arms for Iraq unaccounted for," *Financial Times,* August 6, 2007.
12. Source for small-arms statistics: The United Nations Small Arms Conferences, last held in 2006.
13. Rachel Stohl et. al., "Putting Children First: Building a Framework for International Action to Address the Impact of Small Arms on Children," (paper, The United Nations Conference on the Illicit Trade in Small Arms and Light Weapons in All Its Aspects, New York, NY, July 9-20, 2001).

My understanding of issues in the commercial explosives industry was enriched by conversations with physicist Martin J. Cohen, inventor of the ion mobility spectrometer, which is used to screen for explosives in airports.

Mythic Marijuana

14. Bob McKeown, "Firestar .45: The Tragic Story of One Gun More," documentary, *The Fifth Estate,* directed by Morris Karp, CBC, October 3, 2007.
15. Henry Greely, Barbara Sahakian, John Harris, Ronald C. Kessler, Michael Gazzaniga, Philip Campbell and Martha J. Farah, "Towards responsible use of cognitive-enhancing drugs by the healthy," Nature, December 7, 2008, http://www.nature.com/nature/journal/vaop/ncurrent/full/456702a.html.
16. Martin Booth, *Cannabis: A History* (New York: Picador, 2003).
17. Stephen Kisely, "Applying the Lessons of Tobacco and Alcohol Control to Cannabis," *Canadian Journal of Psychiatry* 53, no. 12 (December 2008): 799.
18. Stephen Kisely, "The Case for Policy Reform in Cannabis Control," *Canadian Journal of Psychiatry* 53, no. 12 (December 2008): 795-797.
19. Wayne Hall and Robin Room, "Obstacles to a Regulated Cannabis Market," *Canadian Journal of Psychiatry* 53, no. 12 (December 2008): 798.
20. Wayne Hall and Robin Room, "Should We Recriminalize Cannabis Use? The Case Against," *Canadian Journal of Psychiatry* 53, no. 12 (December 2008): 793-794.

Masters of Their Universe

21. Anthony Storr, *Solitude* (London: Fontana Paperbacks, 1988).
22. Fumiko Hoeft, Christa L. Watson, Shelli R. Kesler, Keith E. Bettinger and Allan L. Reiss, "Gender differences in the mesocorticolimbic system during computer game-play," *Journal of Psychiatric Research* 42, no. 4 (March 2008): 253-258.
23. Gary Small and Gigi Vorgan, *iBrain: Surviving the Technological Alteration of the Modern Mind* (New York: HarperCollins, 2008).
24. Josh Wingrove, "As search ends, father hardens resolve," *Globe and Mail,* October 27, 2008.
25. Mary Bellis, "Computer and Video Game History," About.com: Inventors, http://inventors.about.com/library/inventors/blcomputer_videogames.htm.
26. Mihaly Csikszentmihalyi, *Flow: The Psychology of Optimal Experience* (New York: Harper and Row, 1990).
27. Sarah Boesveld, "Gadget-savvy but socially inept? Tech may be altering your mind," *Globe and Mail,* October 16, 2008.
28. Sharon Kirkey, "Docs citing e-addiction," *Windsor Star,* March 17, 2008.

How Pernicious is Pornography?

29. David Denby, "Dirty Secrets," review of *Zack and Miri make a Porno,* directed by Kevin Smith, and *I Loved You So Long,* directed by Philippe Claudel, *New Yorker,* November 10, 2008, Arts & Culture section.
30. Diane E. Levin and Jean Kilbourne, *So Sexy So Soon: The New Sexualized Childhood and What Parents Can Do to Protect Their Kids* (New York: Random House, 2008).
31. J. Paul Federoff, "Sadism, Sadomasochism, Sex, and Violence," *Canadian Journal of Psychiatry* 53, no. 10 (October 2008): 637-646.
32. Norman Doidge, *The Brain that Changes Itself: Stories of Personal Triumph from the Frontiers of Brain Science* (New York: Penguin, 2007).
33. Pamela Paul, *Pornified: How Pornography Is Damaging Our Lives, Our Relationships, and Our Families* (New York: Henry Holt, 2005).

"So, Why Do You Write?"

34. Ron Charach, "A Psychiatrist and a Poet," New York University Literature, Arts and Medicine Blog, December 8, 2007, http://med-hum.med.nyu.edu/blog/?p=83.
35. Salman Akhtar, "A Bit of Prose about Poetry," *International Journal of Applied Psychoanalytic Studies* 5, no. 2 (2008): 90-96.
36. Salman Akhtar, lecture, 14th annual Toronto Psychoanalytic Society's Day in Applied Psychoanalysis, Toronto, ON, September 27, 2008.

Don't Call Me White

37. Source on demographics: U.S. Census bureau, August 14, 2008 as quoted by Trish McAlaster in *Globe and Mail,* November 1, 2008

Canaries in the Mind-shaft

38. Ian Buruma, "The Jewish Myths of Asia," *Globe and Mail,* February 20, 2009

It was beyond the scope of the essay to tackle the issues surrounding anti-Semitism in countries where there are very few Jews, such as China, Japan and Southeast Asia. Ian Buruma's article nicely summarizes how "conspiracy theories thrive in relatively closed societies, where free access to news is limited and freedom of inquiry curtailed." He also emphasizes the extent to which European anti-Semitism was transplanted during the process of colonization.

39. *Arguing the World,* directed by Joseph Dorman, (Project of Riverside Film Productions, 1998).
40. There were leading Jewish intellectual influences on public policy long before Milton Friedman rose to prominence. During the Depression of the 1930's and after, a school of New York Jewish intellectuals, whose families hailed from Eastern Europe, became the first working-class voices to pronounce on public policy. These men became public intellectuals, and included Nathan Glazer, Irving Kristol, Daniel Bell and Irving Howe.

Reflections on Jewish Identity

41. Howard Jacobson, *Kalooki Nights* (London: Random House, 2007).
42. Ian Brown, "Reflections on the Big Owe of '08," *Globe and Mail,* October 11, 2008.
43. John Murray Cuddihy, *Ordeal of Civility: Freud, Marx, Lévi-Strauss and the Jewish Struggle with Modernity* (New York: Basic Books, 1987).
44. Ruth Gay, *Unfinished People: Eastern European Jews Encounter America* (New York: W.W. Norton, 1996).

This essay was very much inspired by the intimate live interview of Howard Jacobson which took place at the Annual Cherie Smith Jewish Book Festival in Vancouver, conducted by Eleanor Wachtel, host of the Canadian Broadcasting Corporation series *Writers & Company.*

Timothy Geithner's Jewishness was assumed by many, but even Jewishfriendly websites like Heebz!, Famous Jewish People and Jew or no Jew, which developed a rating scale for rating the degrees of Jewishness of prominent individuals, decided that Mr. Geithner is not Jewish, but rather is a Protestant. This, of course, does not entirely clear the air, since, in the eyes of anti-Semites, this resident of Westchester County and protégé of leading Jewish political figures is viewed as a Jew in hiding, akin to the Maranos of old. Despite the fact that Barack Obama has zero Jews in his cabinet, the traffic in fears about Jewish influence, especially on the internet, may be substantial. On a day in April, 2009, entering the word "Christians" into Google yielded some 43 million hits, "Muslims" yielded 25 million, while Jews produced a whopping score of 55 million hits, "Jewish conspiracy" alone offered a hit count of more than 500,000.

Borat's Inner Jew

42. Jaime J. Weinman, "Did Bunker beget Borat?" *Maclean's,* October 31, 2006.

Bibliography

Akhtar, Salman. "A Bit of Prose about Poetry." *International Journal of Applied Psychoanalytic Studies* 5, no. 2 (2008): 90-96.

Al Aswany, Alaa. *The Yacoubian Building.* New York: HarperCollins, 2002.

Bascunan, Rodrigo and Christian Pearce. *Enter the Babylon System: Unpacking Gun Culture from Samuel Colt to 50 Cent.* Toronto: Random House, 2007.

Bashir, Halima, *Tears of the Desert: A Memoir of Survival in Darfur.* Ballantine, 2008.

Baskin, Bernard. "Escaping 'the sea of chance." Review of *Maimonides: The Life and World of One of Civilization's Greatest Minds,* by Joel L. Kraemer. *Canadian Jewish News,* December 4, 2008.

Bauer, Gabrielle. "Focus on Fibromyalgia." Report, annual meeting of the American College of Rheumatology, San Francisco, CA, October 24-29, 2008.

Bissell, Tom. "The Grammar of Fun." *New Yorker,* November 3, 2008.

Bloom, Paul. "First Person Plural." *Atlantic,* November 2008.

Booth, Martin. *Cannabis: a History.* New York: Picador, 2003.

Brackman, Levi, and Sam Jaffe. "Rabbi is rich." *Harper's Magazine,* December 2008.

Brown, Ian. "Reflections on the Big Owe of '08." *Globe and Mail,* October 11, 2008.

Buruma, Ian. "The Jewish Myths of Asia," *Globe and Mail,* Feb 20, 2009

Cash, Andrew. "Locked and loaded." Special Report: Banning Handguns in Canada. *NOW Magazine,* September 17-24, 2008.

Cave, Terence. *How to Read Montaigne.* London: Granta Books, 2007.

Cuddihy, John Murray. *The Ordeal of Civility: Freud, Marx, Lévi-Strauss, and the Jewish Struggle with Modernity.* New York: Basic Books, 1974.

Denby, David. "Dirty Secrets." Review of *Zack and Miri make a Porno* (View Askew movie) and *I Loved You So Long* (Sony movie). *New Yorker,* November 10, 2008.

Di Matteo, Enzo. "10 reasons we need a national hand gun ban." Special Report: Banning Handguns in Canada. *NOW Magazine,* September 17-24, 2008.

Doidge, Norman. *The Brain that Changes Itself: Stories of Personal Triumph from the Frontiers of Brain Science.* New York: Penguin, 2007.

Eltahawy, Mona. "The opium of the people, and other Arab taboos." *Globe and Mail,* December 30, 2008.

———. "The sister we missed." *Globe and Mail,* February 24, 2009.

Frattaroli, Elio. *Healing the Soul in the Age of the Brain: Why Medication Isn't Enough.* New York: Penguin Books, 2001.

Freud, Sigmund. *The Complete Psychological Works of Sigmund Freud. Vol. 18, Beyond the Pleasure Principle.* London: The Hogarth Press, 1920. Standard Edition. Edited by James Strachey. W.W. Norton, 1976.

———. *The Complete Psychological Works of Sigmund Freud. Vol. 21, Civilization and Its Discontents.* London: The Hogarth Press, 1930. Standard Edition. Edited by James Strachey. W.W. Norton, 1976.

Fromm-Reichmann, Frieda. *Principles of Intensive Psychotherapy.* Chicago: University of Chicago Press, 1960.

Gay, Ruth. *Unfinished People: Eastern European Jews Encounter America.* New York: W.W. Norton, 1996.

Gilligan, James. *Violence: Reflections on a National Epidemic.* New York: Random House, 1997.

Greely, Henry, Barbara Sahakian, John Harris, Ronald C. Kessler, Michael Gazzaniga, Philip Campbell and Martha J. Farah. "Towards responsible use of cognitive-enhancing drugs by the healthy." *Nature,* (December 7, 2008), http://www.nature.com/nature/ journal/vaop/ncurrent/full/456702a.html.

Greenberg, Irving. *The Jewish Way: Living the Holidays.* New York: Simon and Schuster, 1988.

Hall, Wayne, and Robin Room. "Should We Recriminalize Cannabis Use? The Case Against." *The Canadian Journal of Psychiatry* 53, no. 12 (December 2008): 793-794.

———. "Obstacles to a Regulated Cannabis Market." *The Canadian Journal of Psychiatry* 53, no. 12 (December 2008): 798.

Horton, Scott. "Justice after Bush: Prosecuting an outlaw administration." *Harper's Magazine,* December 2008.

Hyde, Lewis. *The Gift: Creativity and the Artist in the Modern World.* New York: Random House, 2007.

Jacobson, Howard. *Kalooki Nights.* London: Random House, 2007.

Jamison, Kay Redfield. *Touched with Fire: Manic-Depressive Illness and the Artistic Temperament.* New York: Simon & Schuster, 1993.

Jarecki, Eugene. *The American Way of War: Guided Missiles, Misguided Men, and a Republic in Peril.* New York: Simon & Shuster, 2008.

Kisely, Stephen. "The Case for Policy Reform in Cannabis Control." *The Canadian Journal of Psychiatry* 53, no. 12 (December 2008): 795-797.

———. "Applying the Lessons of Tobacco and Alcohol Control to Cannabis." *The Canadian Journal of Psychiatry* 53, no. 12, (December 2008): 799.

Klein, Naomi. "Baghdad year zero: Pillaging Iraq in pursuit of a neocon utopia." *Harper's Magazine,* September 2004.

Levin, Diane E., and Jean Kilbourne. *So Sexy So Soon: The New Sexualized Childhood and What Parents Can Do to Protect Their Kids.* New York: Random House, 2008.

Lumpe, Laura, *Running Guns: The Global Black Market in Small Arms.* London: Zed Books, 2000.

Marmur, Dow. "A fight, too, over David and Goliath." *Toronto Star,* January 11, 2009.

De Montaigne, Michel. *Essays.* Translated by J.M. Cohen. London: Penguin,1958.

Nafisi, Azar. *Reading Lolita in Tehran: A Memoir in Books.* New York: Random House, 2004.

———. *Things I've been Silent About.* New York: Random House, 2008.

Nathanson, Donald L. *Shame and Pride: Affect, Sex, and the Birth of the Self.* New York: W.W. Norton, 1992.

Olsen, Norman H., and Matthew N. Olsen. "An inside story of how the US magnified Palestinian suffering." *Christian Science Monitor,* January 12, 2009.

Paul, Pamela. *Pornified: How Pornography is Damaging Our Lives, Our Relationships, and Our Families.* New York: Henry Holt, 2005.

Phillips, Adam. *Going Sane.* New York: HarperCollins, 2005.

Real, Terrence. *I Don't Want to Talk about It: Overcoming the Secret Legacy of Male Depression.* New York: Simon & Schuster, 1998.

Schwartz, Jeffrey M., and Sharon Begley. *The Mind & the Brain: Neuroplasticity and the Power of Mental Force.* New York: HarperCollins, 2002.

Shattuck, Roger. *Forbidden Knowledge: From Prometheus to Pornography.* New York: St. Martin's, 1996.

Small, Gary, and Gigi Vorgan. *iBrain: Surviving the Technological Alteration of the Modern Mind.* New York: HarperCollins, 2008.

Smith, David Livingstone. *The Most Dangerous Animal: Human Nature and the Origins of War.* New York: St. Martin's, 2007.

Smith, Mike. "One piece at a time." Special Report: Banning Handguns in Canada. *NOW Magazine,* Sept 17-24, 2008.

Storr, Anthony. *Solitude: A Return to the Self.* New York: Simon and Schuster, 2005.

Terefenko, Paul. "Harper's dangerous gang." Special Report: Banning Handguns in Canada. *NOW Magazine,* September 17-24, 2008.

Wadud, Amina. *Inside the Gender Jihad: Women's Reform in Islam.* Oxford: Oneworld Publications, 2006.

Index

A Christmas Story, 28
Aboriginal peoples. *See* First Nations
addiction, 71–72, 80–83, 89, 117
AK-47, 26, 31, 49
Akhtar, Salman, 110
alcohol, 71–78, 94, 113, 116–17
American Bureau of Alcohol, Tobacco and Firearms, 24, 40
Andreasen, Nancy, 113–15
Anslinger, Harry J., 71
anti-Semitism: abroad, 123, 177n38; in *Borat*, 164–66; Jewish, 160; in North America, 138–42, 152–54, 147, 159; online, 157–58, 178
Aswany, Alaa Al, 110, 150, 155
Atari, 85
atheism, 168–70
attention deficit disorders, 14, 74, 86

Baron Cohen, Sacha, 164–65
Bascunan, Rodrigo, 27–28, 35
Beck, Aaron, 11, 108, 110
Berlin, Richard, 118–19
bin Laden, Osama, 46, 129
Bloom, Paul, 12
Bloomberg, Michael, 42, 158
Blumenbach, Johann Friedrich, 131
Body Worlds 2, 16, 60–63
Borat, 15, 164–66
Brain that Changes Itself, The, 81, 89, 94
Bush administration, 22, 24, 130, 160
Bush, George W.: on guns, 36–37; as president, 13–14, 67, 126, 128. *See also* Bush administration

Call of Duty, 80
Canada: First Nations of, 29, 136; guns in, 24–26, 31, 33, 38, 79; marijuana in, 68–70, 77–79; politics of, 46, 126; tasers in, 39–44
Canadian Broadcasting Corporation (CBC), 24, 43, 152, 167
Canadian Institute for Legislative Action (CILA), 26
Canadian Shooting Sports Association (CSSA), 31
cannabidiol (CBD), 69. *See also* marijuana
Caucasian, 131–32, 134, 136
censorship, 90, 93, 135
Cheney, Dick, 13, 126, 128
Chesler, Phyllis, 146–47
China, 46–48, 177
chiropractic medicine, 98–100, 104
Chomsky, Noam, 153, 160
Christianity: v. atheism, 167; in *Borat*, 166; early, 51–52, 139, 157; fundamentalist, 63, 146–47; and Judaism, 123, 140, 143, 157

chutzpah, 138–39, 160, 169–70
cocaine, 16, 71–72, 94
Cohen, Martin J., 170, 175
Columbine High School, 14, 35, 86
Conservative Party: under Harper, 126; on issues, 25, 41, 68, 76; v. Liberals, 128, 138
Cover, Jack, 40
Crisp, Brandon, 80
Csikszentmihalyi, Mihaly, 82

Dawkins, Richard, 167–68, 170
Democratic Party, 26, 29, 129
Dershowitz, Alan, 158, 160
District of Columbia v. Heller, 22–24
Doidge, Norman, 81, 89, 94
drugs. *See specific names of drugs*
Drugs, the War on, 69, 71, 78
Dziekanski, Robert, 40–41, 44

eBay, 32, 82
École Polytechnique de Montréal, 14, 37, 43–44
ecstasy (E), 71, 73
Electronic Media Disorder, 86
Eliot, T. S., 117
Eltahawy, Mona, 149–50
Emery, Marc, 69–70, 77–79
Enter the Babylon System, 27–28, 35
entertainment industry, 158
ethnicity: Jewish, 138, 140–41, 152–54, 166; in North America, 15, 124, 156
explosives, 47–48, 129, 170, 175

father, 20, 28, 147
Federal Bureau of Narcotics (FBN), 71
Federoff, Paul, 94
Feinstein, Dianne, 158
fetishism, 28, 94
fibromyalgia, 74, 96–97, 99, 101–105
firearms. *See* gun
First Nations, 25, 29, 132, 136
first-person shooter (FPS) video games, 12, 28, 32, 85–86
flow, 82–84
Freud, Sigmund: Goethe Prize winner, 107; as a Jew, 156, 162, 165; life of, 53, 159; psychology of, 15, 92, 94, 165; quotes by, 12, 16, 110, 119, 159
Friedman, Milton, 140, 177n40
Froman, Sandy, 31–32, 158
Fromm, Erich, 11
Frost, Robert, 117
fundamentalist. *See under names of specific religions*
Gandhi, Mohandas, 80
Gaza, 13, 125, 141, 149
Ginsberg, Allen, 76
Glock, 29, 31
God, 53, 157, 167–71
Goethe Prize, 107
Goldfarb, Edward, 168
Goldman Sachs, 138, 158
Government Accountability Office (GAO), 49
Grand Theft Auto, 83, 85
Green Party, 68
Greenspan, Alan, 127–28, 138, 159
grow ops, 69
gun: control, 19–37, 79, 126, 157; manufacturers, 21, 28, 33, 37; trafficking, 24, 68, 79; violence, 14–15, 21–27, 38–44, 130, 162. *See also specific names of guns*

Halo, 83, 85
Hamas, 125, 129, 141, 149
Harper, Stephen, 37–38, 68, 76–77, 126
Hearst, William Randolph, 71
Helwig, Maggie, 112–13, 116
heroin, 16, 71–72
Heston, Charlton, 29
hip hop, 26–28, 134–35

Hitchens, Christopher, 150, 167–70
Holy Blossom Temple, 60, 161, 167
homeopathy, 98, 100
homicide, 19–25, 51, 147–48, 162
Hussein, Saddam, 46, 129–30
Hyde, Lewis, 139

immigration, 139, 155–56, 164
Internet: addiction, 82–84; anti-Semitism on, 157, 178; drugs available on 77; pornography, 90–91, 94; video games, 80
Islam: in *Borat,* 164, 166; discrimination against, 123, 139, 162; fundamentalist, 47, 51, 134, 144–50, 162; growth of, 142, 153; myths about, 70; orthodox, 155
Israel: anti-: 153; role in Jewish life, 139, 143, 146–47; role in Middle East, 123, 125, 141–42, 148–49, 159–60

Jacobson, Howard, 152–54, 156, 160–61, 178
Japan, 85, 92, 135, 177
Jewish identity: in *Borat,* 164–66; and cultural values, 139, 156–60, 167, 142; and economics, 127, 138–41, 143, 158; of immigrants, 155–56; influence of, 177n40, 178; in *Kalooki Nights,* 152–54
Judaism: anti-Semitism within, 160; fundamentalist, 147, 151; Orthodox, 62, 95, 155, 161–162; Reform, 161; traditions of, 139, 156, 163

Kalooki Nights (Jacobson), 152–54
Kapner, Nathanael,157–58
Klein, Naomi, 129, 160
knives, 19–20

Laing, R. D., 11
lethality, 34, 39, 45–47
Liberal, 127, 138
Live 8, 45
Lowell, Robert, 107, 113, 115, 117–119
LSD, 71, 74

Madoff, Bernard L., 142
Magnum, 28
Maimonides, 141
manic-depressive, 114–16
marijuana, 68–79
Marmur, Dow, 60, 63
Marx, Karl, 153, 156, 165
McCain, John, 14, 126–28
McLuhan, Marshall, 74
mental illness, 23, 58, 113, 118–19
Mexico, 15, 24, 71
Middle East: US involvement in, 125, 129; war in, 70, 141–42, 144, 148–49
Montaigne, Michel de, 172
Mumbai, 15
murder. *See* homicide
Muslim. *See* Islam

Nafasi, Azar, 149
National Organization for the Reform of Marijuana Laws (NORML), 76
national firearms registry, 126
National Rifle Association (NRA), 26–27, 31–36, 37, 158
NATO, 25, 46
naturopathy, 98
New Democratic Party, 68
New England Journal of Medicine, 22–23
No Country for Old Men, 30

Obama, Barack: cabinet of, 178; on guns, 26; as presidential candidate, 14, 127–28, 152; and racism, 29, 136

Ontario Science Centre, 50, 60–61, 63
Oslo Accord, 46

Palin, Sarah: campaign, 93, 127–28; on guns, 32; rumours about, 152, 157
Para-Ordnance, 25, 31, 33
Paul, Pamela, 91–93
Paul, Saint, 157, 166
Pearce, Christian, 27–28, 35
Phillips, Adam, 12, 89
Physicians for a Smoke-Free Canada, 72
Pilates, 100, 103–4
Plath, Sylvia, 113, 116–119
poetry, 107–17
pornography, 90–95
Postman, Neil, 16, 84
psychiatrists, 11–12, 58–59, 106–9

racism, 29, 131–36, 164. *See also* anti-Semitism
rape, 94, 147, 150
religion. *See names of specific religions*
Republican Party: gun-control, 21, 37; v. Democratics, 29; policies, 25, 69, 127–29
rocket-propelled grenades (RPGs), 47
role-playing games (RPGs), 85
Royal Canadian Mounted Police (RCMP), 40–41, 44
Rumsfeld, Donald, 13, 129, 159
Russell, Steve, 85

sanity, 12,
Scalia, Antonin, 27–28
Schneidman, Edwin, 47
Sebastian, Saint, 51–52, 98
self-defence, 23, 26, 157
self psychology, 145
Seung-Hui, Cho, 30–32
sexism, 136, 151
sexual abuse, 90, 146–150
sexuality, 33, 89–93, 145–46, 165
shame and rage, 29, 145–149
shtum, 153–54, 160
Small, Gary, 83–84, 88
Solomon, Evan, 167–68
South Korea, 80
suicide: bombers, 51, 62, 146, 148; and guns, 22–23; risks, 47, 66; of writers, 112–117

TASER International, 30, 39–42, 44
tasers, 30, 39–44, 174
Terror, the War on, 25, 71, 78
tetrahydrocannabinol (THC), 69–70
Thomas, Clarence, 25, 28
Tikkun Olam, 139, 160, 167
tobacco, 71

Ultimate Fighting Championship, 16, 42
UN (United Nations), 45, 70
United Kingdom (UK), 19–20, 69, 153
United States (US): drugs in, 68, 71, 77–78; guns in, 22–29, 33; tasers in, 41, 43; and the Middle East, 129–30, 142–43; race and, 14, 136; video games in, 80; weapons in, 47
Uzi, 31, 33

Valentine, Saint, 51
video games: addiction, 80–88; first-person shooter (FPS), 12, 28, 32, 85–86. *See also specific names of video games*
Vietnam veterans, 24, 70
violence: and drugs, 70–71; gun, 25–27, 36, 130; knife, 19; in media, 30, 38, 85–87; in the Middle East, 14, 147, 149, 172

Virginia Tech (Virginia Polytechnic Institute and State University), 23, 30–31, 36, 38
von Hagens, Gunther, 50–51, 60–63
Vonnegut, Kurt, 52

Walther pistol, 31
war: Civil, 29; Cold, 129; in the Middle East, 26, 47, 130, 148; World War II, 53
Wordsworth, William, 52
World of Warcraft, 83
World Trade Center, 149

Xbox, 80

YouTube, 82, 140, 150

Zamora, Isaac, 21
Zonis, Marvin, 144